For more (fun)
+ fun, Kristine

Man - Woman Relationships Made Easy

♂ ♀

Kristina Catalina, R.H.

International Promotions
San Diego, California

Man-Woman Relationships Made Easy
Copyright 2003 by Kristina Catalina

Quotes attributed to Victor Baranco, Ph.D.
are reprinted with the permission of
Lafayette Morehouse Inc.
and Cynthia A. Baranco, Ph.D.

Cover Photography by Jeff Kasselbaum, Carlsbad, CA

Shoes from Cedros Soles, Solana Beach, CA

Published by
International Promotions
9921 Carmel Mtn. Rd. #337
San Diego, CA 92129
858-490-1411

ISBN # 1-57901-053-9

Cover Design by Marcia Perkins

FOREWORD

♂♀

If you've been searching for a philosophy that will enable you to have more joy and happiness in your relationships – congratulations. This book will change all your relationships. What you have in your hands is solid gold.

What a wonderful gift this book is for the men and women of today. The simple fact is that most men and women have little idea who the other sex really is. This keeps us from fulfilling our own dreams of glorious, intimate and connected relationships.

Why are there so many failed relationships? At school we were taught the three R's and left to figure out relationships on our own. That's a little ironic when we consider the importance of the topic. How can we participate in a truly profound and satisfying relationship with anyone if we're not educated to appreciate the distinct nature and needs of who they are? This holds true whether we're talking computers, gerbils or the other sex.

Man-Woman is the great teacher of the art of relating. It's so very enticing. We never had to think about whether or not we want to get involved in this game; one day it just happens, and we're in it, anxious and eager, fascinated and afraid. There is just something so delicious about the possibility of a real love-affair, a genuinely intimate relationship that we come ready to play. But there's an admission fee, if we're serious about getting the prize. We have to be willing to step outside of our own existing point of view   As long as we insist that we know how the other sex should be, and that they're wrong for being the way they are, our relationships will prove to be a source of frustration and regret.

What you are now holding in your hands, as laid out in Kristina's own simple, yet rich style, is a bridge that brings every relationship closer together. But there's much more – there's the possibility of far greater access to your own growth and purpose as an individual.

This book is something else. For all who are ready to bite their teeth into something sweet, crisp and juicy, here it is. Kristina Catalina is holding up a wonderful carrot that will lead people to a place where they can at last be intimately and profoundly related, both to themselves and to each other as men and women, in a way that perhaps they've only dreamed of before.

Martin Lyons
Man-Woman Seminar Leader
and Relationship Coach

PREFACE

♂♀

The R.H. on the back cover, following the author's name stands for, Relationship Humorist. This designation represents what Kristina is – she is the first Relationship Humorist, and deserves this title because she has uniquely applied humor to a serious and sensitive subject.

This book is the culmination of 24 years of work and study in the field of man-woman relations. For the past 18 years her passion has been focused on the imponderable dynamic between men and women. Out of that effort she discovered some simple but powerful distinctions that would instantly alter anyone's relationship. She knew this was the work she was here to do, but needed to fully experience all these distinctions for her self before she could share them with the world.

Previous to this revelation, she was one of the millions of women who was frustrated and confused about how to relate with men. She had just ended another relationship with a great man and once again thought it was his fault. It seemed odd to her that after many years of relating with men, she had never come across any information so simple yet profound. It wasn't until after years of further study that she realized how bizarre it was that so many people were unaware of how simple it was to win with the opposite sex.

For the next several years she talked with hundreds of men and women about these insights and learned how to integrate these precious pearls of wisdom into all her interactions.

Once she saw that these distinctions would consistently and easily empower anyone relating to the opposite sex, it became very clear to her that she was here to impart this information to men and women who were open, willing and ready to experience the kind of relationships we all dream about. When she saw these simple ideas create miracles and transform many relationships over and over, she was compelled to write this book.

This book is written descriptively and is not meant to be prescriptive. Kristina is not a therapist or a psychologist. She is a cheerleader for people to have more fun and connection in their lives. She's not telling you what she thinks you should do, but what you can do. Whether it's between spouses, dating partners, associates at work, acquaintances or family, there are always opportunities for fun or failure. Paying attention to the differences she is delineating between men and women will enable you to avoid many of the failures, and increase the opportunities for fun.

The first 26 chapters of the book will give you major insights into the perfection of our differences. You can start at the beginning and read straight through, or you can open the book anywhere and pick a chapter. You will gain a deeper understanding of who YOU are and how to play your side of the man-woman equation. The second half came from a transcript of a Man-Woman course she taught in San Francisco. It will drive home a lot of the ideas and distinctions that are discussed in previous chapters.

It is by intention that certain truths are repeated throughout the book. Some are so simple that most people pass them by thinking they couldn't make that much of a difference. Not so. So Kristina drives some of these points home again and again. Keep an open mind and trust that your understanding of these distinctions is all that is required to have the kind of relationship you've always dreamed of.

There are no accidents. This book is in your hands because, whether you are conscious of it or not, you are still searching for answers to the mystery of how to have success and FUN in your relationships with the opposite sex. Simply allow yourself to feel the essence of what you're reading. Trust and know in your heart that successful relationships are not only possible, they are much more probable with this information. When you understand and embrace the perfection of how different we are, you'll begin to see the light at the end of the funnel. From today forward you will see the opposite sex in a new light, a light that honors and celebrates our Creator's brilliance in making us so different.

Part two of this book is a reproduction of the verbal presentation of Kristina Catalina's relationship seminar, *Clearly Related.* In this half of the book you will notice a less formal format. Our intent was to maintain the playfulness with which Kristina conducts her seminars as well as give you an opportunity to get to know her better.

INTRODUCTION

♂♀

This book is about man-woman relationships. It offers many precious secrets that will clarify why so many relationships are less than satisfying. It solves many of the mysteries of the man-woman relationship, and once you discover how to play the man-woman game, it will open new doors for you and you will have more fun with the opposite sex. In fact it can change your life by improving all your relationships, including your romantic, your partner, your business associates, your family members, and your friends.

Relationships can be awful or awesome. Whatever yours is, it's your creation. Here you will discover the incredible effect women have on men and on every relationship they're in. You will also discover how to use your power in attractive and compelling ways. You will learn how to have win-win relationships. This cliche might sound trite, but it's critical to a healthy, long-lasting relationship. When everybody wins, everybody is happy, more creative and more productive. Happy relationships have a ripple effect and add to the well-being of everyone they touch.

Here you will discover a major misunderstanding about who you are dealing with regarding the opposite sex and how it has caused you to miss many opportunities, but from this book forward you won't have to live with misunderstanding and missed opportunities.

Kristina uncovers distinctions about men and women never revealed before. She demonstrates how kind, loving, empowered, successful **and** feminine women can be with any male they encounter. Men will learn how easy it is to win with women. This book offers some very simple tools for men that will have women smiling from ear to ear.

This is the Relationships 101 handbook and the advanced course all in one.

Acknowledgements

A very special thanks to:

- ♥ John Catalina for loving me unconditionally and for being such a loyal friend. Thank you for the incredible journey we've had. You helped me find my wings to fly and you will be in my heart forever.
- ♥ Robin Mayfield for encouraging me to write this book; for being there with me every moment, and for bringing so much joy to my life. You are an angel with a very special heart.

My deep love and gratitude for my many teachers, "the men and women" at "MORE U".... for showing me the power and the gift of enjoying each moment. Especially Victor Baranco for his profound insights about how to have MORE JOY in life. Without his brilliant teachings I would not have the unique knowledge I needed to write this book, however much of what I share in this book is not necessarily what he taught.

Victor Kent for your willingness to play with all sides of me. Anchor Man for loving my "Kris-ness" and for your very wise words. Timothy Brewer for the invaluable lessons. Ted Crisell for your generosity. Mighty Kim for your trust in me Vinnie and Indy for being the most precious four-legged friends a girl could ever have to love.

And many thanks to my wonderful friends and family for always believing in me, and for their unending support and inspiration. This book is for you and for the well-being of the entire planet.

DEDICATION

I dedicate this book to my parents,
Pat and Doug Craig,
for teaching me the importance of
'Kindness.'

Contents

Dedication...1

Chapter 1
Man-Woman is the Best Game In Town 3

Chapter 2
The Master Game 11

Chapter 3
What You Think Your Relationship Is 17

Chapter 4
Who Runs the Show and
        Who Eats the Popcorn 23

Chapter 5
Women Start, Steer and End Relationships
        with Enigmatic Drive 31

Chapter 6
Love is an Inside Job 39

Chapter 7
The Real Truth About What's Attractive
        to a Man... 47

Chapter 8
Trippin' the Love Switch 55

Chapter 9
Asking Powers 63

Chapter 10
Men are More Than Willing 71

Chapter 11
Are You Talkin' To Me?! 79

Chapter 12
Guess Who Wins? 87

Chapter 13
What Women Do 24/7 95

Chapter 14
Forgive Women for They Know Not
What They Do 101

Chapter 15
Straight Talk about the 'C' Word 109

Chapter 16
Men Have Given Up and Women Are Resigned 117

Chapter 17
Men and Women are the Same
in Different Ways 125

Chapter 18
Got Intimacy? 135

Chapter 19
The Difference Between Sex and Sensuality 143

Chapter 20
Tame the Blame Game 151

Chapter 21
Spontaneous Funbustion 159

Chapter 22
Women Want Sex, Food and Baubles 165

Chapter 23
Present and Great Lovers 173

Chapter 24
The True Power of a Woman 181

Chapter 25
Turning a Nightmare into a Dream 189

Chapter 26
Everything Matters 195

PART II 202

There
is
every
reason
to be
enthusiastic.

Attributed to
Victor Baranco, Ph.D

Chapter **1**

Man-Woman is the
Best Game in Town

Anytime a man and a woman are together, the potential for magic or mayhem exists. Our world has yet to accept the very special gift we've been given in being so different. We have not learned to utilize the awesome power available to us in the man-woman dynamic. There are many games to play in this world, but nothing can bring more joy than the man-woman game. There is no finer playing field than relating with the opposite sex to experience all aspects of love and life.

In order to effectively relate to one another, we must understand and appreciate, the underlying makeup of men and women. Women bring the appetite and desire to the planet. Men bring their capability to produce. In order to move efficiently around the game board of man-woman, we need to recognize women are better than men in the area of desire, and men are more effective than women in producing to satiate those desires.

We were not created different by accident. The plan has always been perfect, but we have resisted the perfection of our differences. This resistance has been the source of the majority of man-woman breakdowns.

Women are best at what they want. Men are best at making it happen. Women are the ones who wanted indoor plumbing. Women are the ones who wanted beds up off the floor. They wanted a roof over their head. They wanted more blankets and food for their children. Women are the ones who wanted transportation and markets to do their shopping. They wanted materials to make different clothes; ones for winter and ones for summer. Women have always wanted their basic needs of food, shelter and clothing met. Women wanted, and men provided. Life was simple. It's not to say that women didn't make things happen along the way. The truth is, women made everything happen simply by expressing their desires. They wanted more pleasurable experiences.

Times have changed, and the women of today need to allow men to be men, and empower them to do more of what they do best. Men want women to know they are completely capable of producing whatever women want and need, as long as they are given the opportunity.

Over the past several decades, women have taken on more of the male role of producing. If this continues, we will end up with too much male energy on the planet. The planet doesn't need more male energy - it needs more feminine energy.

Women are coming into their power in new and wonderful ways. It's time for them to pull back from producing so much, and move more into directing. This will allow men to support women in moving things in the direction of the feminine. This will bring balance back to a world where the feminine energy is wanted and needed.

Romance goes out the window when women take on a man's role. In the times when chivalry was alive and well, women were definitely more feminine. They were happy to be female. They played their part with grace and ease. Men were heroic and romantic. They were happy to court women and women were delighted to be courted. Can you imagine if women were galloping off to slay dragons for their men? When women do the man's job, it leaves little room for men to be their heroes. There is no game to play, or dragon to slay. It results in no romance.

Mark lived in Texas with Allison. Allison had a vacation magazine that had a beautiful picture of an island with gorgeous turquoise waters. She lit up every time she looked at it. One day Mark said to her, "Would you like to go there?" She said, "Yes, that would be like a dream." That was all she said. The next day Mark bought tickets for them to go. She was simply enjoying the picture and thinking about how much fun it would be to go there. She was not trying to manipulate him in any way. This is different than a woman who asks, "Would you take me there?" or, "Why can't we go?" There's no opportunity for men to be the hero if women get their own 'production' muscle involved.

When a woman expresses her desires, she is giving her man a clear message how to win with her. He must pay close attention to what she says she wants. If he doesn't take her clues he will be penalized at some point. Women can't stand it when men don't listen to them, especially, when they feel it's important. By the way, everything a woman says is important. It would behoove a man to remember that women only want things that will make them happy. If a man's primary goal is to make his woman happy, it will cost him big time if he misses what she wants by not listening to her.

If a man doesn't listen to the direction a woman suggests, she feels totally discounted. Nothing is worse for a woman. A man immediately goes to the doghouse for this. A woman will decide he is not fun to play with, and the relationship will potentially go down hill from there. Not following a woman's lead can be detrimental to the health and vitality of a relationship. When a woman's desires are paid attention to her light will shine and her love will easily flow toward her man.

Some women keep the majority of their desires from their man. Women don't realize that the more they want, the better it is for men. If a woman is nice, in addition to having a big appetite, that's even better. Men want to produce big. They are not afraid of women who have big appetites and big dreams. They actually find it attractive. A woman with big dreams means the man has the opportunity to be a big hero.

Men will never have a chance to be a hero by second guessing women. This will never work. It always bothers women. Women know men think we aren't as smart as they are about certain subjects. But women are clear about things that are truly important to them, and would like men to take them for their word. They usually give men an 'X', when men judge women for not being clear about what they are saying. It makes women feel frustrated. They will quickly lose interest in furthering the conversation.

An example of second-guessing would be where a woman might say, "I want those little purple pens for my invitations." He says, "What do you want those for? Those aren't the right color to get. They won't work either. You need to get this kind and this color." Men should know that women say what they mean, and mean what they say, even if a man thinks it doesn't make sense.

Women have been put down by men for much of their life and, unfortunately, don't stop to handle the criticism in the moment. However, they will get their revenge by holding out the fun in some way. They simply refuse to enjoy themselves. If men would simply adopt a woman's goals without questioning them, they would experience a much happier woman, much more of the time.

It's a huge burden for women to always have to know what they want. It's a lot of pressure to have this responsibility. Some women have not exercised the 'knowing what they want' muscle. They don't always know what they want in the next moment.

Part of a man's job is to help her discover her desires. Women love it when men 'run menus' for them. Running a menu is the same as offering a list of options for her to consider. It's like window shopping or going through a catalog. Sometimes women just need the spark of new ideas to inspire them. When men run menus, women can be more at the effect of their circumstances, which is something women love. It allows men to do the thing they love, which is to be at cause of the situation. Everybody wins this way.

When a man gives a woman a list of options, all he has to do is watch her face, and then pursue the thing that makes her face light up the most. If her face lights up, she has connected with something she feels would be fun. If a man is on the phone with her, he needs to be listening intently for any positive feedback. A man's best bet is to start in the direction that feels best to him. If a woman changes her mind along the way, it's best to change with her and follow her lead. It won't cost him, and he'll be rewarded for being willing to go with her flow. That's always the perfect solution.

There are many books to read that claim to show you how to have fulfilling man-woman relationships. I honestly haven't found any that comes close to the simple truths found in this book. If you are going relate with the opposite sex, and your goal is to have fun, it is a must to honor and embrace the powerful distinctions that exist in our differences. The most important distinction being that women are the *appetite* and men are the *producers*. Learning this piece alone will insure that your travels in the world of man-woman will lead to a lot more fun and a lot less frustration. It's the best way to travel in life, period. It produces the most fun, the most clarity, and it makes the most sense.

Become more of an observer of your relationships and your life, and you will quickly see how simple relating with the opposite sex can be. When you come up against challenges, simply observe where you may be responsible, acknowledge it, and move on. Nobody ever has to be wrong! It's a much cleaner way to play man-woman.

Take a look around you and you will see the result of a woman's appetite. All the houses, cars, clothes, restaurants, and shopping centers were brought into existence by a woman's desire. Women want, and men produce. You don't see too many women building cars, or roads, or houses and shopping centers. Women want experiences they are pleasured by. They wanted prettier cars, smoother roads, bigger shopping centers, and finer dining. And men, bless their wonderful hearts, brains and muscles, produced it all. Men are amazing creatures who love to produce. Women love to want - it's a perfect dynamic in a perfect world.

Men long to produce for feminine, happy and receptive women. It's important for women to remember that men would love the opportunity to be their hero. Women have to give them the chance. Women have to become more receptive to convey their softer, more feminine side. They can get what they want without getting the ol' crowbar out. The more women allow themselves to be happy, open, feminine females, the more men will be inspired to listen to them, love them, and adore them. Men can only adore women who are adorable. The question, is have you been adorable lately?

Adopting this model of man-woman allows both sexes to be fully expressed and honored. This model is simple. It's clean, fun, fast and honors everyone. It allows men to be manly - the kind of men that women are always saying they want. And it allows women to be vulnerable, soft, feminine, and still powerful - the kind of women that men say they want.

Try this model out. You will see instant results - guaranteed. It's so simple, and it really is this easy! Give up the effort and struggle of playing man-woman any other way. If you choose to play with the other half of the planet, you'd be wiser and happier when you play from your blanket of power - blue blanket or pink blanket?

There is
no end to
how good
life can be
if you find
it good in
the first
place.

Attributed to
Victor Baranco, Ph.D

Chapter 2

The Master Game

Man-woman is called a master game because you can never master it. It is never ending and always evolving. You can never get ahead of it, because as you evolve in the game, the game continues to evolve around you. You never know what direction it will go next. It is ever-changing, like life itself. Unlike learning to play a violin, where you can learn enough to become a master, you will never learn enough to master this game. So if you decide to go forward in a man-woman relationship, you will need to embrace that it's a life long process. Man-woman is the most rewarding, satisfying, and thrilling adventure we can ever hope to have.

The only way to play is to play 'full out'. You only go around once in this body of yours. We all know life is not a dress rehearsal, so if you're going to play anything worth while in life, why not play it as if your life depends on it. Your health, aliveness and sanity are totally affected by how you live your life. No one is forcing you to play man-woman. Either play the game 100%, or don't play at all. Playing it any other way, than with your total heart and soul, will produce a mediocre existence - a life less than spectacular.

Much to everyone's disbelief, there are couples who are living happily ever after. There are relationships that are filled with bliss, and joy, and laughter. It's only because these people have chosen to make it a priority to move through whatever challenges they have, quickly and with love. This gives them access to the joy that's always available when they live in the moment. They are freed up to enjoy the process of relating and have given up kicking and screaming all the way to paradise.

When you begin a relationship with someone, you'd better be happy with who they presently are. If your plan is to change them in anyway, it will be drive you both to an early grave. Put your attention on what is working, what you want, and give up any complaining. Whining women and complaining men quickly drain the juice of everyone they touch. The quickest way to add more juice to your relationship is to cancel your membership to the Victims & Whiners Club. Women who whine are on the top of a man's turnoff list. There's no constructive use for whining and complaining. It simply makes you unattractive. Give it up immediately! Life could be over in the next moment – and you don't want your last breath to be a whine.

♂♀

Problems are always the opportunity for more growth. Knowing that you can resolve anything in your relationship can be very liberating. When the goal of happiness has top priority, there is nothing that cannot be resolved. It doesn't matter if the situation is good, bad or ugly. Decide to choose happiness over being right and alone. It's a decision you can make when you see how pointless and senseless it is to choose anything else. Life is too short to waste time arguing. When your goal is happiness, you will automatically be drawn to resolutions that will bring you more of it. Lighten up and get over yourself. Many couples have told me how important humor and laughter is to their relationship, especially when there are serious challenges.

How many of you are still beating yourself up for past failures? It's important to remember those failures happened in the past. If you are still hanging on to the past, let go of it. Today is a fresh new day. There are definitely times to be more serious and mature than others, but for the most part, we all need to lighten up.

♂♀

Learn to play and the drama goes away. The Man-woman game has more opportunities for fun than any other area of your life. You can get away with being childlike and playful with your partner more than anyone else. When was the last time you gave yourself permission to be childlike? Playing has the ability to break the tension any time you want to end the drama you're in. It works any time you're just plain bored. To dance in an elevator or break out in song in a grocery line, would lighten up everyone's day, especially your own. If you want to let go of your drama, it's as easy as making the decision to play more.

Play clean. It's the only way to play. Playing clean means to honor and respect yourself and your partner. It means to have integrity in your relationships and with yourself. It's important to remember, that no matter how your partner is playing his hand, what counts, is how you are playing yours. Playing clean with everyone you meet will give you peace of mind, diminish your personal drama and have you sleep soundly at night. If you're a clean player in life, your partner and friends will feel safe around you. This will win their respect and trust.

No one is wrong and no one is to blame. You can't do it wrong! You are the master of your world. Even if you mess something up, you learned from it and will hopefully do it different the next time. Worrying what other people think is one of the reasons we avoid being ourselves. The more we're willing to express ourselves, the more we have to share with others. Learn from your mistakes. Don't beat yourself up with them.

♂♀

Adopt an attitude of gratitude for all the delicious women and gorgeous men on this planet and you'll instantly have much more to be happy about. When you focus on what will make you happy, you will quickly see there are a lot more things to smile about than you ever realized. They've been there all along. It's just that your focus hasn't been on what makes you happy. If your goal is happiness, be grateful for everything.

The more present you are to everything and everyone around you, the more you will notice the humor in life. You can let yourself be delighted and grateful, instead of perplexed and disappointed, by the differences in men and women. If you choose to be delighted, you will tap into the biggest resource imaginable for continuous fun and laughter. You get to choose to create happiness or not. It's always been your choice.

Trust that the physical universe wants to give you what you want. The harder you struggle to find the perfect relationship, the faster you push it away. When people struggle, they are communicating on an unconscious level, they don't trust the perfect relationship will happen for them. Stay open to all opportunities that come your way and believe that your dreams will come true. Anytime you have doubt about achieving your dreams, you prevent the universe from giving you what you want. Even happiness will stay away if you don't trust and believe you can have it.

If you want more happiness adopt more winning viewpoints - Life is good. I love my wife. My husband rocks. My relationships are the best. It's this simple. To have more happiness, be aware of what you focus on, because what you focus on will expand. Focus on the good things in life. It's so simple to have relationships that are filled with goodness.

All you have to do to be happy is keep your attention on what you love. Look at what you love in everything you do and love will permeate every corner of your world.

Go out and enjoy yourself, or stay in and enjoy yourself. Whatever you do, enjoy yourself *now*! You won't get another chance to enjoy this moment. Let yourself go. Give yourself room to be the happiest person you know. Happiness is infectious. It's what the world needs now! Give happiness a chance and great relationships of all kinds will follow.

Being
ruthless
in the
pursuit of
pleasure is
commendable.

Attributed to
Victor Baranco, Ph.D

Chapter 3

What You Think Your Relationship Is

Your thoughts are the most powerful driving force in all your relationships and in your life. The way we choose to see our relationship creates the way it works. All you need to do is look at what you have and you will see the results of your thinking. This being true, you can't afford to have any negative thoughts. Negative thoughts bring negative experiences. The more you dwell on the things you don't want, the more you attract them. It's important to monitor your thoughts daily to be sure you're attracting more of what you want instead of what you don't want. Your thoughts are writing the script for your relationships and your life.

Think about what you want and simply watch it show up. If you're in a relationship, it's because your thoughts have created it. For those of you who are single, your thoughts have manifested you being single at the moment. There's nothing wrong with being single. It is simply the result of what you've had your attention on. When you feel it's time to truly have a relationship, your thoughts will shift to the picture of being in one. Putting attention on these new thoughts will begin to manifest situations that will bring a relationship to you.

Our beliefs can make or destroy a relationship. All our relationships have the potential of being outstanding. Every moment of every day you are creating how you want your life to be. When your attention is focused on what you love about your life, more good will appear. The same thing occurs when you focus on what you don't like. You will end up having more of what you don't want.

If a woman thinks that she's not enough for her boyfriend, those thoughts will eventually bring about the end of the relationship. On the other hand, if she sees herself as the perfect woman for him, this will create the momentum for the relationship to move in a positive direction.

If you think you are a winner or a failure - you are right. Most people don't believe that creating the life they want could be as easy as being conscious of the kinds of thoughts they're thinking. They don't want to accept this level of responsibility. However, if you believe that someone outside of yourself is responsible for your life, you have given all your power away. In reality there are no winners or losers. There are only the conversations people have about themselves and their lives. If you think you're a failure, your attention is focused on failing. You will bring circumstances into your life which reflect this kind of thinking. The opposite is also true. If you think you're a winner, you are. In reality, you're not a winner or a loser. You are a human being having human experiences that mirror what you're thinking.

Stop trying to fix life - find it good *now*. It's quite simple. If you want a relationship and a life filled with good experiences, you have to start with finding the good in what you have *now*. You have to want what you have before you can have what you want. If you are trying to fix or change something because you don't like it, you'll end up bringing that negative vibe to your next adventure.

How many times do you hear people say they want to move because they are sick of the traffic, the noise, the people, the weather, etc. They are trying to fix their life by leaving a situation they dislike. They don't realize that leaving something they view as negative will have them bring more of that same negative experience with them. When people want more good experiences in life, they need to move forward with the attitude that life is good.

Relationships mirror where we are. When you begin to observe your relationships, you will start to notice they all reflect your current thinking. If you're upbeat, chances are you will attract upbeat people in your life. It's fun to be with upbeat people, especially if you are one, because it's like being with yourself. On the other hand, if you are depressed, you will quickly attract others who have similar negative dramas. This is another reason to watch your thoughts and behaviors because you always and only attract from the frequency you're in. It's called the law of attraction. Likes attract likes.

What you don't like about yourself will show up everywhere. As long as there are issues you haven't learned to accept, you will continue to bring in experiences to force you to deal with them, accept them, or let them go. There is no way to avoid this, as this is how we grow. If your relationships aren't working well, you need to look at where you have not accepted yourself. It's never about the other person, although many people try to work out their issues by blaming the other person. This kind of logic leads to a dead end every time, because ultimately, no one is responsible for your issues except yourself.

What you like in your partner is what you like about yourself. Everybody enjoys spending time with people who vibrate at their same frequency. It makes them feel connected. Sometimes we see things in our partner we really love and wish we had. The truth is what you respect and admire in your partner reflects your traits as well. You may not think you have them, however if they weren't part of you in the first place you'd never see them. Notice the traits of the people you love and admire and you will begin to see more of who you really are.

Relationships are the opportunity to grow. Being in a relationship is the greatest self-development course there is. They are the opportunity to learn that when you love and accept yourself, you will have more capacity to love and accept others. Relationships of all kinds force people to look at their issues, whether they want to or not. Having someone to work these out with speeds up the growth process tenfold. Yes, they can be a lot of work, but with the distinctions you are learning in this book, they can be the greatest adventure God ever gave us.

♂♀

Time to wake up! It's a huge step for human beings to learn to become conscious every day. The survival of our planet depends on people learning to focus their attention on the quality of thoughts they have. People need to become aware of the power their thoughts have in creating their relationships. The condition of the relationships in their world is the direct result of their thinking. Each of us needs to begin taking responsibility for our actions and our thoughts.

You created it - you can change it, starting *now*. To sit around and feel guilty for the way your relationships are would be wasting more time. What's done is done. There's only *now* and what you choose to do with it. If it's not working, change your perspective *now*. It was created by you and your partner, therefore, it can be changed by you as well. Life is too short and precious to endure relationships that aren't what you want. Creating positive relationships can start with a single powerful thought. It is your choice. Give your time and attention only to the thoughts that will bring you more happiness and you'll be happier. That's how thoughts work. What you think about is what you bring about.

Be in control of your life - know every thought matters. People who think their lives are out of their own control need to wake up. They need to take responsibility for the fact that they are the ones who created the mess in the first place. When you know your life is your creation, it becomes easier to take control of it. Since you are powerful enough to create it one way, you can just as easily create it another. The truth is, you've always been in control. The problem is, you have never accepted this. No one is writing the script of your life other than you.

Change your thoughts and write a new script, if that's what would make your heart sing. Take care of today and the future will take care of itself. There's no time like the present time to change your thoughts. Stop worrying about the future and concentrate on enjoying whatever you're doing now. Everybody knows there's no future, only consecutive moments of *now*. *Now* is the only reality. What are you thinking right *now*?

The fun
is in the
commitment;
it doesn't
matter
if you
win or lose.

*Attributed to
Victor Baranco, Ph.D*

Chapter 4

Who Runs the Show and Who Eats the Popcorn

On some intuitive level women sense they run the show in the man-woman game. They don't know however, how accurate this feeling is. If women actually accepted this to be true they would relate with men in a much more effective way. The world would look completely different if women realized their hands are on the steering wheel.

A woman's biggest problem in relating to the opposite sex is assuming men know more about women than they do. It's very difficult for women to comprehend that men simply do not understand the world of women. Since men understand so much of how the rest of the world works, how could they not understand women? How could they not understand the very creature that has more of an affect on them than anything else?

This misunderstanding has been a major cause for much of a woman's upset, anger and disappointment. Most women are of the opinion that men rarely get it right with them. Women assume men know what women want. They don't realize that men will never have the opportunity to get it right if women don't learn to speak up and tell them exactly what they want. Men fail to get it right simply because they don't know what 'right' is.

You don't find a woman kicking a puppy across the room for peeing in the corner. They know that puppy's don't understand that this is unwanted behavior. However, women constantly beat men up for doing things men don't know they're not supposed to do. Men become frustrated because they were never taught the right way to do it. Women make men wrong for not getting it right over and over again. You hear women say, "Oh, he's so dumb". They say this like he's wrong for being this way, instead of realizing that he is completely uninformed about what women want.

One of the great things about men is that they come one way - willing. Relationships will change for the better very quickly when women realize how willing men are. They are dying to know what on God's green earth they can do to make women happy. If women realized how eager and willing men are to hit a home run for them, they would stop making men wrong. It's time, ladies, to give this one up!

Women have to remember that even though they want many of the same things, every woman's individual needs are different. The trouble is men relate to women as if all women come from the same mold. Women don't realize that if they are not continually informing men of their specific needs, there's no way for him to know what she wants and therefore no way for him to win. The majority of a man's information about how to succeed with women comes from the last woman he was with. Otherwise he learned most of what he knows from other men. This could be a frightening thought because these men are, most likely, no more qualified in the art of the how to please a woman.

Women need to see men in a totally different light because men are really on our team. They are not the enemy. If women could see men as simple, uncomplicated, loving creatures who are simply cruising the planet looking for some way to win, women would realize how much fun they could have with men. They would see that men love to produce for something as simple as a smile on a woman's face. There's nothing more gratifying for a man than a happy woman.

A great example of this was when I was driving in downtown Seattle in rush hour traffic. I had stopped at a busy intersection. I thought my parking break was on so I leaned down to release the handle and, by mistake, popped the hood. There was a man in a big cement truck right next to me who saw the hood pop up. He could see me through the sun-roof. He saw how flustered I was. I smiled at him over what I had just done. He said, "Hold on, I'll get it". He jumped out of his huge truck, slammed the hood back down and got back in his truck. I was so tickled I just ranted and raved and thanked him profusely. He knew how pleased I was. He was my hero and he drove away feeling like King Kong. Men are very willing to please, especially when they see a damsel in distress.

♂♀

A woman's most powerful tool is her mouth. Unfortunately, women underestimate in a very big way, the effect of what comes out of it. This was one of the most powerful realizations that I ever had. I was 36, cute, powerful and fun. Or at least I thought I was fun. Since I had these qualities it was a mystery to me why I couldn't keep a man around for an extended period of time. The problem was, I had no idea how my words came across to men. I had no idea of the negative effect of what was coming out of my mouth. I spoke to men like they understood the world of women. If women knew how they sound to men, they would

25

put more attention on how they are speaking. It's not just the words that get women in trouble it's the intention behind what they are saying that affects men the most.

The degree to which men can't interpret what a woman is saying is unfathomable to her. Women are aware of a multitude of things at the same time because they are multi-tasked creatures. They track life at many different levels. It's not the same for men. When women speak to men expecting that they should understand everything, men feel intimidated and somehow know they're not going to win. Women communicate their disappointment and anger more than they realize, which makes a man feel like a failure.

Men have a built-in barometer. This helps them to know the difference between yuck and yum. You can't fool a man about how a woman's communication feels to him. One of the tools they have to decipher the world of women is their gut. It's their barometer and if it feels bad to them, it's most likely that the woman intended it to feel that way. Most women don't take responsibility for the fact that they can have this much of an affect. When they refuse to accept this, they lose their power.

A woman's words affect men in subtle but substantial ways. When women are unhappy and communicate from a place where they think it's a man's fault, men automatically feel like a failure. Even if a woman doesn't think she meant to make him feel bad, her true intention is demonstrated by what actually happened. If he feels bad from something she said it's because she wanted him to. You can count on a man's barometer to be right on the mark. They simply respond to what women are putting out. You can trust a man to tell the truth about how it feels to him in the moment, because it's not in a man's nature to have women be wrong.

You hear woman saying how insensitive men are when actually the opposite is true. Much to a woman's surprise men are way more sensitive than they realize. Men are super sensitive; they just don't show it the same way women do. They've learned to hide their feelings because it isn't safe to express them. They put their feelings last because they think they need to be the hero, the one who takes care of everyone else first. When women realize and accept that men are very sensitive creatures, it will behoove them to be more loving in their communications.

Women are not in touch with what it means to be a woman in this day and age. They have spent so much of their recent focus on making it in a man's world they've become out of touch with their true nature and power. Women have become super-producers because they needed to show the world they could make it on their own and be self-sufficient.

The world of women has evolved rapidly over the past 50 years. We are now beginning to place more emphasis on the softer feminine side of what it means to be female. If you look at the trends in women's fashions today, you will notice they accentuate the softer, more playful side of women, instead of the masculine, business look. It's a softer, sexier and more sensual look. The new fashions acknowledge where a woman's true power is, and at the same time honors her completely.

Women have the titles, careers and salaries like men, but they don't have the men or the romance they want. All you have to do is watch the news and see women everywhere demonstrating they can make it in a man's world. For many women, making it in a man's world isn't all it was cracked up

27

to be. Talk to women who are at the top of their field and they're happy about what they've achieved. However, if you ask them if there's anything missing, more often than not, they will say, "A man!" Romance, intimacy and love are missing. If they're honest with themselves they may even admit they are bewildered by it. They don't quite know why men are absent from their life but know they have something to do with it.

The feminist movement definitely served its purpose. However, women of the 21st century are beginning to find that making it in a man's world by operating like a man, is really the booby prize.

It's now time for women to act more like women. They need to learn to use their power in a more feminine, kind and gentle way, and produce the same kind of results through the power of attraction. This is about *Womanism* not Feminism. In any relationship, toughness is no match for tenderness. Women will be pleasantly surprised by the positive responses they will immediately get from men as soon as they understand how to use the power they were given at birth in a more feminine way. When women shift their focus from manpower to woman-power a whole new world will open up for everyone.

When women realize they run the show, while the men get the popcorn, relationships will transform over night. This is not just about transforming your personal intimate relationship, it's about transforming any relationship they have with the opposite sex. This includes their fathers, sons, husbands, ex-husbands or employers. When women begin to see men with this new understanding of the effect their feminine power has, it will be freeing beyond their wildest dreams. Relating with the each other will open up a whole new way and will produce more fun than they could ever imagine. And what do we want more of from our relationships? We want more fun, laughter, and lots of it!

A woman
keeps the
species
going by
having men
want to be
involved
with her
desire to
gratify
herself.

Attributed to
Victor Baranco, Ph.D

Chapter 5 ◉)

Women Start, Steer and End Relationships with Enigmatic Drive

The title of this chapter is the most misunderstood statement of what actually takes place in man-woman relationships. If you think its some other way you are mistaken. Women have been waiting for men to take the first step, when the truth is women are the ones who start the ball rolling.

When women initially hear this it can be rather frightening. For women to believe they have this much power and have started every relationship is quite a shock. They usually don't like it when they hear this because it puts the responsibility totally on the woman. Women don't realize, however, how simple it can be to relate with men when they surrender to this truth. They don't realize that all they did in the beginning to catch their man was approve of him. They acknowledged and appreciated whatever he did and this was all it took to get the man's attention.

It all starts with a woman's desire and intention whether she is conscious of it or not. She has rehearsed over and over in her mind what kind of man will make her happy. When she is hunting for a man out in the world her light is on. When she sees a man who interests her she simply 'drops her hanky'. She lets him know in some subtle and sometimes not so subtle ways that she approves of him and uses several body language gestures that communicate her interest.

Men can't help but respond to women especially when she's being attractive. They do, however, have a choice how they respond. Women are always communicating something. They are always putting out some kind of signal that men constantly try to tune into. Women need to be clearer and more aware of what they are putting out. Men want nothing more than to win with women. To achieve this they read everything about a woman from the tone of her voice, to her body language, to the look on her face.

Many times when there is a group of women out socializing men will feel more comfortable approaching the one who is having fun, rather than the one who is more physically attractive. To get a man's attention, it's as simple as glancing at him with a smile, or saying something nice to him. That's how women 'drop the hanky'. It doesn't matter if the woman is shy or a ball of fire. What matters is how nice she is.

Kind is good too, and playful is even better. A man said to me recently that he didn't care how attractive the woman looked. If she wasn't kind or playful he wouldn't be as interested. Men fall for women who are happy and nice to them. Men are like weather vanes. The weathervane doesn't think about what direction it is going to go; it has no process. When the wind changes it follows automatically. When a person or situation becomes fun, men automatically move toward it without even thinking.

Women get a bad rap for getting all dressed up to go out on the town, and then unkindly reject a man's acknowledgment when he tells her how beautiful she looks. Women do this if a man doesn't fit her initial picture. This is mean behavior and has men wondering why they bother approaching women at all. The end result is that men sit back and just watch what's going on, leaving women to wonder what's wrong with them. No one wins this way.

To steer a relationship means to direct it toward what you want. What do you want? Where do you want it to go? Do you want marriage? Do you want to date? Do you want a lover? If you want it to go in a particular direction, you must be clear what you want. How does your relationship look right now? Is it going where you want it to go? All these questions need answers in order to get what you want.

This should be a huge eye opener for women. I had always been pointing my finger at the men in my life, blaming them for anything that wasn't working. I didn't notice there were three fingers pointing back at me. When I first realized that I was steering the relationship I was not thrilled. It meant that I had also been responsible for how my past relationships turned out.

It is important for women to realize they have always been in the driver's seat. For too long they've been operating as if someone outside of themselves has been in charge. Being in the driver's seat means you have everything to do with the shape your relationship is in. When women see this and own it, they can begin to take responsibility for the direction of all their relationships. They can also begin to humbly take responsibility for their past relationships as well. They were either a nightmare or some level of fun. Whatever they were, it was the result of how the woman steered it. It's what she

33

intended consciously or not. Women are always steering whether they want to own this or not. So where do you want to drive today? Ecstasy Avenue or the Nightmare on Elm Street?

Women steer relationships into ecstasy when they're happy and into a nightmare when they are not. It's really simple. If a woman is having her needs met, she's happy. Everyone is winning, especially her man. If a woman isn't getting the kind of attention she needs or wants, she and the relationship can be a nightmare.

♂ ♀

The first major mistake a woman makes is when she expects a man to know what she wants. It's amazing to me how many women really believe that men know what women want. The truth is, many women don't know what they want for themselves, and if they don't know, how can they expect men to figure them out and get it right?

Figuring women out is not in the cards for men in this lifetime. For a woman to assume that men know what's going on with her is pure insanity. This kind of thinking sets both sides up to lose. The bottom line is, women have to tell men exactly what they want. Even more important, they have to tell them in a nice way!

Relationships go down hill when women start to disapprove of their men. When a woman no longer approves of her man, she begins to gather all sorts of evidence to validate her beliefs. She will end the relationship when it becomes too much work. There's a point when a woman clearly knows she is not going to be fulfilled by her man. She will know she won't achieve the goals that are important to her by staying with him.

Women will become upset and angry when they realize they can't trust a man to keep his word. When she is let down and continually disappointed she decides he is too much work. When she knows she can't trust him she loses respect for him. If a woman loses respect for a man, it's over. She's loses her energy and her juice for him and knows it's time to move on. From this point on men know they can't win. They respond to a woman's disapproval by leaving. Why would a man want to be around a woman who is constantly finding him wrong? Keep in mind, men don't leave if women are having fun and approving of them.

It goes like this. Joe hadn't been getting much approval around home and went off one evening to get a video. When he was walking into the video store a woman was coming in behind him. Joe held the door open for her and she gave him a big smile and an appreciative thank you. The approval felt so good to him that he decided to get into conversation with her and then followed her around the store. He wound up spending the evening with her because she was simply nice to him. Men never leave when women are treating them nicely; they only leave when women take their approval away. Once a woman has taken her approval away, she is saying that he is no longer worth her energy. She is done!

A lot of people stay far too long, "thinking and hoping and wishing and praying, planning and dreaming" that things will be different. Get a grip! It's not going to change until you do. Sometimes when relating becomes too much of a struggle, all it means is your lessons are complete with this person and it is time to move on. I've seen in my private coaching practice time and again, a lot of unnecessary hardship for couples thinking they have to stay in the relationship when it's clearly over. It's all right to move on and nobody has to be wrong.

People don't have to take their friendship away when a relationship ends. Too many times people end relationships that were once wonderful and never see the other person again. They have all these reasons why they cannot be friends. How silly is it to completely stop loving someone you once loved? People would benefit by having more friends of all kinds in their lives, not less. You never have to have less love for a person. You are simply changing the form of the relationship. You can still remain friends and honor and celebrate each other.

In the end, women have the power to steer men into many different kinds of relationships. Good relationships aren't only romantic ones. You can have best friends, dance partners, movie buddies, or business partners. Remember men just want to win and have their production used in an attractive way. Women have the power to put their hands firmly on the steering wheel and drive any relationship in the direction where everybody wins.

When loving
is more
than enough
you're
eligible to
fall
in love.

Attributed to
Victor Baranco, Ph.D

Chapter 6

Love is an Inside Job

Since time began we've been searching for happiness and love outside of ourselves. We've looked for other people, things and places to fulfill this never ending quest. It is not until we finally realize that we are the only ones who can fulfill this need, that we can stop searching. Only then can we truly have the kind of magic we all dream of having.

The sooner we come to accept the realization that there is no one more capable of making us happy than ourselves, the more likely we'll be able have fulfilling man-woman relationships. No other human being is capable of making you happy; it's not their job. You are responsible for your own happiness. Your boyfriend isn't, your lover isn't, your boss isn't and your mother-in-law isn't. You are also responsible for your own sadness and madness. You choose how you want to experience whatever happens to you. Life is 10% what happens to you and 90% what you do with it. So what are you doing with it? What is your attention on? Is your attention on how gooooood your life is right now? Or is it on what you don't like? If your focused on what you don't like you will quickly attract more of it. The only way to have more good in your life is to find your life right, RIGHT NOW! Not later!

Women think it's a man's job to make them happy. Think again! Get hold of yourself! You are in deep doo-doo, girlfriends, if you think a man knows what on earth to do to make you happy. Give that one up immediately! You give all your power away to a man if you are counting on him to be in charge of making you happy. Make yourself happy first and then anything a man does, in addition, will be a bonus. It will be a bonus for a man as well, because men love to do things for a woman who is already happy.

I had a client named Sally who sat around many evenings and weekends waiting for her boyfriend to call to invite her out. Instead of having a good time with her own life Sally was waiting for to him to make her happy. When he didn't call when she thought he should her light began to go out. She finally decided to do some coaching with me and quickly saw the importance of being responsible for her own happiness. She began filling her time with all the things she loved to do and shortly thereafter, her boyfriend picked up on her positive energy and started calling more often. She was a lot happier because she wasn't depending on him for her happiness. Remember men are like weathervanes and automatically move towards fun.

Successful relationships are the result of knowing that YOU are in charge. Once both parties accept this responsibility there will be no reason to complain, blame or whine. This will quickly take your relationships to a whole new level.

It's easy to forget that you are in charge of your own happiness. It's all about exercising a new muscle we haven't been using. We've been playing the 'blame game', which is a much lower level way of playing in life. It gives you very weak muscles to maneuver in life. You give your power away when you let someone outside yourself control of your happiness. When you put someone else in charge, you destroy your ability to create what you want. Notice people in the world who have lots of friends and are wonderful to be around. They are people who know they are in charge of their own happiness. They know they are responsible for the way they respond to their circumstances and are rarely victimized by life.

People think worrying will make a difference in their circumstances. Otherwise, why would they worry? What worrying does is perpetuate what you are worrying about. Worrying communicates to the world around you that you don't believe you and your life are perfect. Ultimately people believe that life won't turn out the way they want it. They think if they worry long and hard enough it will change everything. Worrying is a waste of your creative energy. It gets you nowhere. So don't worry; choose to be happy. Exercise your 'happy' muscle every chance you get. After all, life is not a dress rehearsal.

Happy relationships are created when you love yourself first. To love yourself first means to be selfish in the good sense of the word. If we are incapable of loving ourselves, how can we love another? It's impossible for a man to have a successful relationship with a woman who doesn't love herself. The same thing applies for a woman who wants to fall in love with a man who doesn't love himself. We do not have magic wands that can make our partner fall in love with themselves. It's an inside job. You have to love yourself first.

We have to honor ourselves - not judge ourselves. Each of us has to learn to accept, allow and love ourselves for all of who we are. No judging allowed. When you judge yourself and tell yourself you are somehow not good enough you become no fun to be around. You become work for your

41

family and friends. And if a woman doesn't love herself, a man knows there's no way he can turn it around. Honoring yourself means giving yourself permission to speak up for what you need and want, for what supports you. If you don't honor yourself no one else will.

If you think that being in a relationship will make you whole and complete you are sadly mistaken. Being whole and complete means you love yourself just the way you are. No matter what anybody else thinks about you, you need to know you are a good person and are doing your best. When you give up worrying what other people think you will show up in life as a complete person. There is much less work to relating when you know you are whole and complete. You will start living in a place of love and harmony inside yourself. You will see that the problems you think you have with your partner are actually opportunities for you to work on your own issues.

If you're ready to love yourself, start by loving and accepting your body first. Everyone in America has some sort of body issue. We spend billions of dollars, which is an understatement, trying to 'fix' our bodies so that we will love them. Stop the insanity and save your money. This is the biggest issue for men and women regarding self-love. We need to stop looking outside for approval. Our job is to learn how to give it to ourselves.

If you don't love your body, don't expect your partner to. Women look in the mirror and no matter how beautiful they may be, only see what they don't like instead of what they do. A woman's body is similar to a man's car. It can never be too sleek or sexy. If you can't love your body the way it is now, begin by learning to accept it. Find something that you like, put attention on it, and you will find more to love.

One thing a man must never do is to say anything negative about a woman's body! This would be similar to a woman's negative reaction to the size of a man's 'goldmember'.

When women doubt their attractiveness they become unattractive. There's nothing more unattractive to a man than a woman who puts her body down. It turns him off completely. Here he is, simply looking to enjoy being with her, and she throws out a negative comment about herself. All of a sudden any turn-on that had started goes flat and out the window.

True attraction has nothing to do with what you look like. You've seen babe beautiful at the bar who fits all the right pictures, but clearly acts in a way that shows she doesn't really like herself.

It's not about what's on the outside that attracts a man. It's all about whether her light is on from inside. If a woman's light is on it doesn't matter what she looks like on the outside. And you can't fool men. They may ask the pretty ones to dance but nine times out of ten they won't be taking them home. Pretty women have to learn, sometimes the hard way, that just being pretty doesn't cut it. Nice is what counts. Nice is a woman who loves herself first.

I lived with a couple once where Roger kept telling Lisa that her butt was too big. She started thinking she was unattractive and her butt kept getting bigger. She exercised and dieted furiously to no avail. Then she went off on a Caribbean cruise with her mother for 10 days. She ate the whole time and came home more slender than when she left. She realized while on the trip with her mother that there was no conversation that made her feel unattractive. As soon as she was back in Roger's world again her butt resumed it's larger size. Shortly thereafter she woke up one day and decided she wanted to be with someone who loved her for who she was, regardless of the size of her butt.

Everyone must know someone who has done one plastic surgery after another. The sad thing is they will probably never be satisfied with any of the results. They will always think they need more because their basic conversation is one of disapproval. They haven't learned to like themselves just the way they are. Make changes only if you approve of your body in its current state. Otherwise you are always fixing something you consider bad. You will never be satisfied if you can't find yourself right the way you are. Do it because you want to, because it would make you feel better, because it would be fun and because it would make you happy. Just make sure you love yourself before you make the changes. If you are trying to fix something bad your attention is on the bad, and everyone knows what you resist is what persists.

Above all, don't do anything to your body for someone else. If they don't love you for the way you are, why would you want to be with them in the first place? It's okay to want more of whatever you want in life. Just make sure you are happy with how it is first!

Attractiveness is to be so confident that you have time to be truly interested in someone else.

Attributed to
Victor Baranco, Ph.D

Chapter **7**

The Real Truth About What's Attractive to a Man

Most women are unaware of the impression their communication makes on men. They usually talk *at* men, instead of talking *with* men. This kind of interaction never works with men and has them feel unimportant. Unfortunately, men rarely give women an effective reality check on how their communication comes across. If women only knew that the basic nature of a man was his willingness to please, women would make it a point to communicate in a much more attractive way. They would talk in a more sensitive way which would have men be a lot more at ease.

Women have missed the point if they think what's attractive to a man is only skin deep. It may be a bonus to be born beautiful but just because a woman has a pretty face, it doesn't mean they will endure a long lasting relationship. A lot of times being born beautiful can be more of a problem for women, especially if they think it's the most important thing to a man. If a woman doesn't develop her inner beauty the relationship doesn't have much of a chance.

What's truly attractive to a man, and to anyone for that matter, is a woman who has a positive attitude about herself and her life. Women are always doing everything on the outside to make themselves more attractive but neglect the inside. No matter how beautiful a woman is, if her attitude is negative or fearful and she is being a victim in her life, her physical beauty is not going to cut it with a man. In order to bring out her inner beauty, the only thing a woman has to do is keep her attention on whatever makes her feel good in her life. Men are repelled by women who are negative about their life. They know if a woman is negative, they're not going to be able to change her. They won't even want to try.

What's important is your attitude about your life and how you are living it. It is so simple to be attractive to a man. No matter what you look like, where you live, what you drive, or what kind of work you do, if you love yourself, you are attractive. If a woman accepts that she is a sensual creature and gives herself permission to be a woman, or a lover, or a mother - that's attractive. You don't give a man any room to love you if you are putting yourself down in any way.

Every woman has the potential to be beautiful and sensual and we all have our own way of expressing it. Giving yourself permission to be a sexy, sensual, shy, adorable woman is attractive. A woman becomes beautiful when she knows in her heart she is never wrong for how she chooses to be. When she accepts herself fully she does not concern herself with what other people think.

Women get cheated out of living a life that's full when they don't let themselves be who they want to be. Women have to realize they are so much more than their body. They have to realize their bodies are only a vehicle to move around in. It is not who they are. Women who know they are more than their bodies are much more attractive than those who don't. When you know this you will become freed up and more fluid in life. It's sexier and more inviting to a man. So what if you are 10, 20, 30 pounds over weight. Do you love your body? Are you having fun in it? If you aren't, you won't be sexy. You can have an extra 100 pounds and be incredibly sexy, but only if you love it.

I had a male client once who said he could never be attracted to a woman who was hugely overweight. I gave him an assignment of going to hear the awesome blues singer, Etta James. Etta was larger than life in many ways. After watching her sing for several hours, my client was blown away by how attractive she became to him. What he realized was that she loved every inch of herself and that made her completely sexy. This proved my point that men are attractive to women who love everything about themselves.

Women often complain about their jobs, their bodies, their men, and their hair. Women underestimate the affect of their complaining. They think if they are complaining in the presence of a man and are not asking him to fix it, there is no problem with complaining. Women need to know that men never like hearing women complain. In fact, this is one of the more repulsive things women do around men. Men like to see women happy. If a woman complains frequently and there is no invitation for a man to help fix the problem, it makes him feel terrible. It's not any fun for him because when women aren't happy, men don't win. Complaining is NOT attractive behavior.

♂♀

There's a great song by Jewel that says, "In the end only kindness matters". There are many opportunities at every moment of the day to be kind. We overlook many of them.

When it is genuine and given freely with no expectations, it is kindness from the heart. Whenever I'm in my car and someone looks over at me, I always make sure I look the person in the eye and smile to let them know they matter. It makes me feel good. I feel more loving and therefore I am more loving. And when I'm more loving, I become more attractive. Saying kind and thoughtful things from your heart goes a very long way. Are you practicing kindness from a loving heart?

What you give out is what you get back. When you are in a place of appreciation and gratitude whatever you say will be met with a positive response. What do you want to come back to you? If you want good to come your way you need to be sure what you're saying feels good to you first. An ungrateful attitude is a recipe for not having what you want in life. It is much easier for a man to respond to a woman who is practicing an attitude of gratitude.

Appreciate who you are and make sure you inform your face. Women don't realize that what they are thinking shows up all over their face at every moment. Every lovely, or not so lovely little thought, is right there for the world to see.

Sam knew when he and Sally decided to get married he wanted to make her happy for the rest of their life. Then one day Sam belches when they're out with a group of people for dinner. Sally immediately went into her head thinking "Oh no, not that. He's like my ex". Sam sees this disgusted look on her face and asks, "Are you all right? Is everything OK?" She is thinking all sorts of negative thoughts but says, "I'm fine". Sam is now thinking he is crazy because her face looks negative all of a sudden .

No matter how pretty a woman may be, men can take one look at the expression on her face and immediately want to go in the other direction. They know trouble is on the horizon when women have 'that look'. The good new is, when a woman starts having a good time it will transform her face in seconds.

Most of the clues men use to know what's going on with women are the ones written on her face. They see it and they feel it. Appreciating the moment is an instant ticket to having your face be more inviting and attractive. Your face lights up when you're happy and it goes out when you're not.

The way to a man's heart is not only through his stomach. The one thing men get very little of is acknowledgment and approval. Women don't even have to go to the kitchen and a man could be very happy. If you listen to the women in the world talk about their men, it will be apparent they are not ranting and raving about the wonderfulness of their men. There may be a lot they like, but fail to acknowledge because their attention is on the negative. It's much easier to talk about the negative because it has become a habit to talk this way. Women mostly talk about what is wrong or not working.

There are a lot of unhappy women out there who don't know how simple it is to get a man's attention in an attractive way. Women don't know they can have everything they want. What it's going to cost them, however, is enjoying their life NOW. They have to pay for it with their pleasure. It is about exercising a new muscle, the 'Are you happy now?' muscle.

Appreciate, approve and acknowledge in a genuine way. This is the biggest 'ah ha' for all the women who have participated in my workshops. This is one point you do not want to take lightly. Grab a box of tissues and contemplate your past relationships with the following in mind:

All it takes to make a man happy is to give him the 'AAA' treatment – appreciate him, approve of him and acknowledge him. Acknowledge him for anything about your life, your car, your home or your relationship. Appreciate whatever he may have done for you lately, however small it may be. Approve of him by blaming him for whatever good you have in your life. This simple formula can transform your relationship overnight. This alone is worth the price of this book.

So many women walk around in wonderful homes that their men have worked hard to produce and rarely say thank you. They don't express their appreciation for how good their lives are. Tell your man you appreciate having him in your life. Do this every day. It will change your life completely.

Believe your man is willing to give you what you want. Men come one way and that is willing! They are dying to know what on earth they can do to make a woman happy. This is one of the things that frustrate men the most. They know that most women don't have any idea how willing they are to please. Men would be so much more empowered to produce for a woman if she would acknowledge and appreciate what he's already done for her.

A happy, satisfied and gratified woman is the biggest inspiration for a man to produce more. One of the great tragedies of life is that women have never understood this. Men do it all for women. If women would be delighted by the simple things in life and let men know how much they appreciate them, they would inspire men to be their greatest. Behind every great man is a satisfied and gratified woman. That's attractive.

A feminine woman is a woman who enjoys the ride. Being attractive to a great man is as simple as being thrilled with your life and everything in it. Put your attention on what you <u>like</u> and let your joy spill over on any man that comes your way. Men won't know what they did to deserve such joy from a woman, but all will be well and more good will come.

The word
surrender
exists
because it's
an experience
everybody
wants to have...
under the
right
conditions.

Attributed to
Victor Baranco, Ph.D

Chapter 8

Trippin' the Love Switch

As you can see on the cover of this book, the control panel called "women" has many buttons, levers and dials. Unfortunately, the instruction manual was never written until now. For men this book is the "How To" on what you need to have a woman fall in love with you every time. This will teach you what to do with all her buttons, levers and dials (BLDs). Actually, it's not about what to do with her BLDs, as much as it is to simply pay attention to them. This should be a relief for most men. Women will adjust their buttons, levers and dials when women want to, not when men want them to.

Women want men to honor and appreciate everything about them. Women want men to love ALL their buttons, levers and dials. The BLD's consist of her body, moods, randomness, way of communicating, behavior, monthly mania, desire to shop, desire to snuggle and cuddle, desire to be heard, her need to want what she wants ONLY when she wants it, her friends, family, emotions, changing her mind, her need for truth, honesty, and desire for unending attention. If she feels any of the above is neglected, some part of her will shut down and go away. Too much neglect of her BLD's will cause a woman to say NEXT!

Women want men to acknowledge their intelligence and wisdom. Women know they are smarter than men, but most women have a hard time owning this because they've never been truly acknowledged for how intelligent they are. Women don't miss a thing. How could they? Look at all their BLD's. Women have much more access to the world around them because all their BLD's are tracking devices. They pick up on minute details every moment. Women are very smart, smart enough to be dangerous if men don't pay attention.

Women want to feel connected to their partner. Connecting is what it's all about for them. What is the point of life if we're not connected? To be connected with a man gives a woman a sense of safety and security and a feeling of being home. Women understand mankind was created to experience life in connection with one another. Being solo in this world is not natural. If we didn't want to be with each other, there would be no point to living. The importance of connecting is what drives a woman to find a man.

Women want men to fully accept what they do in life. One of the things that women love most about men is when they get totally behind whatever she is doing. It makes a woman happy when she can freely pursue her own goals, knowing that her man is behind her 100%.

Women find it very irritating when a man tries to compete with her. They don't want to play this man's game. Women can be open and appreciative of men's creative contributions as long as they are forwarding what she wants. Women may not approach a project in the way a man would, but want to have their own experiences to learn from.

Women want men to hear them, feel them and know them. For a woman to fall in love with a man she has to know she can trust him. What enables a woman to put down her guard and begin to trust a man is when he is being attentive and genuinely interested in her. It is a major turn on for a woman to have this kind of quality attention. Women love it when they are the focus. Women think they are more interesting than anything else on the planet anyhow, so for a man to be captivated by who she is and what she has to say is considered one of the better forms of foreplay by most women.

Being heard and understood by a man is very important to a woman. Most men don't listen to women. They don't know how. They don't think it's important and have no idea how much it means to a woman. Many times just knowing that the man heard what a woman said, by his acknowledgment of what he heard, will make the difference. It makes a woman feel like he has really paid attention. She feels acknowledged and complete, which is a major step for her to feel connected.

Women want men to listen to them; not fix them. Men want to see women happy. When they aren't happy they want to automatically fix whatever is wrong. Women want to be heard and not necessary fixed when they are talking about their problems. Many times they are looking for a sounding board - nothing more.

A good rule for women to follow is to set the stage before they begin to talk about their problem. Tell your man you'd love it if he would simply listen and not feel the need to fix anything at the moment. This gives a man the direction he needs to know what to do next. They always want to know what women want not what they don't want. It's uncomfortable and not fun for a man to listen to a woman's problems. It is important to make sure he feels appreciated for doing so. This will ensure he will be more willing to do it again in the future. Men like cycles where they know they can win.

Women are interested in the quality of time spent together not the quantity. The thought of being in a committed relationship is frightening for most men. To be in a committed relationship men have to give up the one thing they cherish the most; their freedom. It is true many women are high maintenance and require a lot of time and attention. Men don't realize, however, what really interests a woman is the quality of time spent with them, not the quantity. Quality time is when a woman feels his attention totally on her; when there are no meetings, no phone calls and no interruptions. Quality time is when there is nothing more important than the two of you being together. Quality time is when a man drops everything in his life and takes time to be fully present with his woman.

Women can experience a quality moment from a hug, a kiss or a few precious words. These things can make her feel connected, appreciated and loved. The most important thing for a man is to be present to her in order for her to feel connected. She also wants to feel he enjoys simply being with her.

Women don't need to spend hours on end with men. Too much time with men without some kind of contact with another woman can wear a woman's battery down. Men don't need to be afraid that women will take all of their precious time. If they are willing to give women quality attention a woman can be happy for days.

♂♀

Women love men who are honest & truthful. This is the clincher for women. For women, it's one strike and you're out! It is too difficult for women to be with men who are not honest with them. Women become crazed when a man is dishonest more than anything else. They can't be on guard wondering whether or not they can trust what he is saying. That is torture to a woman and no man is worth that to her. If a woman catches a man in some kind of lie, it permanently damages the relationship. It may take years for her to forgive, and possibly never.

It insults a woman's intelligence when a man isn't honest with her. A woman's intuition is one of her greatest gifts. Women can tell when a man is not telling the truth. What irritates a woman the most is when a man thinks he's pulling a fast one on her. Women are not dumb. They can sense and see way more than men realize. If she knows he is lying to her she has to protect herself. She takes herself away and her light goes out. This is the last thing women want to have happen. A woman wants to be open and free to give herself fully to a man. However, there is no way this can happen if she senses her man is not being truthful. He may get certain parts of her, but he won't get the best parts. He won't get all the fun BLD's and that will be his loss.

A woman wants a man to trust that he can talk to her so that he is heard as well. However, women haven't always made it safe for men to be honest with them. If a woman criticizes a man every time he tries to tell her something, a man will not feel safe to be straight with her. Women need to listen to men and really hear what they are saying. They need to know whatever they are saying is 100% true for them in that moment. A woman may not like it but if she defends or resists what he is saying, it will not be safe for him and he will likely withhold in the future.

If a woman is ever going to have her man be open and honest, she will need to open up her heart, listen more intently and have some compassion. Women have to learn to forgive men for past mistakes. A man on the other hand, has to have the courage to tell it like it is, take whatever wrath may come his way, and acknowledge he was wrong. If he was wrong and his woman was hurt, he needs to apologize and be sincere about it. If a woman continues to beat him up he'll never improve.

When a man meets a woman on this level it opens her heart to fall in love. Everyone needs someone to share their secrets with. Women would love it if men would share their secrets with them. Men would get big points for being this open and honest with women. Everything changes for a woman when he's willing to lay all his cards on the table. When she knows she can trust him, she feels safe. When it's safe in a woman's world all her buttons, levers and dials are free flowing and happy. This enables a woman to finally surrender to a man.

Women
are very
clear about
what
they want
from
whom.

*Attributed to
Victor Baranco, Ph.D*

Chapter 9

Asking Powers

One of our greatest gifts is the gift of choice. We get to choose moment by moment what we will do with our lives. Life is for the asking as they say. We are always asking for some thing. Most people don't realize how true this statement is. We think our circumstances just happen.

Everything we have in our lives come from our thoughts manifesting into reality. What have you been thinking lately? If you have clear thoughts about what you want and believe you can have it, you can. You can live a life where you direct the circumstances or you can live a life where the circumstances direct you.

Women have a difficult time asking for what they want even though it's more permissible for them in today's world. Unfortunately the majority of women still find it uncomfortable to ask for what they want, especially if it's from a man. Many women don't even know what they want. They haven't had enough practice because they weren't given the opportunity to speak up and be heard, let alone ask for what they want. A woman's self worth issues have had a major impact on her ability to honor her needs.

Women were brought up in a world where it was best to be seen and not heard that has changed. When I was growing up I was taught that to be a good girl meant don't talk too much, stay clean, and don't be a bother to anyone. I was told to be polite at all times in adult company and only speak when spoken to. There were many rules about talking. I was also taught not to be greedy and to simply be grateful for what I had. It was a world where women were not honored for their huge appetites and desires.

Female baby boomers were raised to put men on a pedestal, have them think they were the boss, and never offer their opinion unless asked. It was the time of 'Father Knows Best'. Women were taught to do whatever it took to get a man and keep him. Women are now changing their thinking and breaking out of their silent mold.

One of the breakdowns in man-woman relating is that women haven't been asking men for what they want. They haven't asked men because they're afraid they might have to owe him some 'favor' in the future. Also, when women have asked in the past, they've done it in a way that has not inspired men to do anything. Because of this, most women's reality is that men don't want to give them what they want.

It's not that men don't want to take care of women, it's because woman have asked in a way that wasn't attractive. They asked in a demanding way and became impatient if he didn't respond quickly enough. They think it's a man's 'job' to make them happy. One thing is for sure about men; they never move into action when women get the crowbar out. Unfortunately, men have gotten a bad rap for this and it hasn't been their fault. Men literally lose all their energy to produce for a woman when it doesn't feel like fun.

One of the biggest problems women have in understanding men stems from the fact that they really don't believe men want to give them what they want. Women don't realize how their beliefs about men have contributed to their needs not being met. They don't understand that men will never be successful with women until they figure out what women want.

Women have learned to do it themselves and haven't asked for help. They have been so frustrated dealing with men, that it has become much easier to simply do it themselves or go without. Even though there are a lot of capable men around, many women are hell bent on not using them.

We live in a male-dominated society that is beginning to listen to what women have to say. If women want men to be more available and interested in what they want, they will need to talk to men in a more attractive way. Women need to realize that men are standing at home plate waiting to hit a home run for them. However, if they keep throwing those curve balls to them, men will keep crying 'foul'.

♂♀

If you want to have more of what you want in life it will be as simple or as hard as you make it. We can all be pretty stubborn at times. We love to hang on to our stories and share our dramas. What would we have if we didn't have our drama? Perhaps we'd have more of what we really want. However, until we are ready to give up our drama, we will continue down the same dramatic path. Our lives become dramas mostly because we enjoy the story we have made up about it. I invite you to make up a new drama - one that includes what you really want. How novel would that be? The truth is,

65

it's never going to change until you change. The more you resist your drama by wanting it to be some other way, the more it will stay the same.

It may sound too simple, however, if you decide to love yourself instead of the drama you've created, it will be a huge step toward manifesting what you want. When you don't love yourself you are basically communicating to the world you can't have what you want, you don't deserve it and you are definitely not worthy. It takes the simple act of loving yourself, to produce an affect that is far-reaching and very profound.

When you love yourself and know love is what and who you are, it's much easier to have anything you want. Why? Because your lack of love for yourself is the only thing that's in your way. It's the thing that cuts you off from the source of your power.

There is a new gym that all women should join immediately. It's called the Nice Muscle Gym. It's where women develop their 'nice' muscle, which is the most powerful muscle to have. Of course men could join this gym too. Women, however, are the ones who could benefit the most with this type of training.

Men rarely wake up in the morning thinking how they can ruin a woman's day. For women, however, this is not entirely true. If women are still upset from something a man did the night, or day, or week, or month before, they will continue to start their day with a less than loving heart.

One of the wonderful things about men is they will forget any bad time they've had for the past week or month, if all of a sudden their woman is being fun again. All a woman has to do is show a man a little 'nice' and he's ready to play. Women are the one's who usually hold grudges. This is a shame because grudges are not only a waste of time but they make women look older, meaner and a lot less attractive.

Exercising the 'nice' muscle is as simple as finding something good about whatever is presently happening. Put your attention on the positive aspects of the situation that has you upset. Don't go immediately to blame. Look at what you had to do with how it turned out. Take responsibility for your part. Look for a solution where everyone can win. Take the path of love and fun instead of the path of separation and the 'uglies'. The 'ugly' muscle always wants to kick in. We've used that one so often it comes on automatically without even thinking about it. It's the one that produces the same old drama - the stuff we don't want.

Exercising the 'nice' muscle is the way to get more of what you want. Use the 'nice' muscle to make YOU feel good. If you don't make yourself feel good, do you think somebody else will want to? The juicy result of using the 'nice' muscle is that everyone around you gets to benefit. It's always a win-win situation!

Love what you have first and you'll have more of what you want. If you don't love what you have now, do you really think you are going to love whatever is coming down the pike? I mean, let's get real here ladies and gentlemen. One of the ways a woman can inspire her man to want to do more for her is to show him how much she loves what he's already done for her. It never feels very satisfying to give to someone who doesn't appreciate what they already have. What's great about loving what you already have is that it will insure your happiness whenever you want it. Then it won't matter what comes next. You are already happy.

♂♀

This brings me to the conversation of desire. If there was no desire on the planet, life as we know it, would not exist. It is our birthright to desire whatever we want. Desiring is good. Desire makes the world go round. Desire gives everyone an opportunity to play on the game board of life. If you stop desiring you may as well be dead. Goethe said "Whatever you can do, or dream you can do, you can. Boldness has genius, power and magic in it. Begin it now."

There is a purpose behind men and women being created with our individual and distinct desires. Anytime a man and a woman are together, their powerful dynamic has the potential to produce miracles. Whatever this world needs to be a healthy and vibrant place to live can be available when we harness the power available in the man-woman dynamic. We have to learn how to play man-woman the way it was designed.

Women need to know what they want. Learning to receive starts with asking for what you want. Many women may say they know what they want and ask for it. However, some still say they don't get what they want. The missing link is learning to receive. We can want all we want but if we aren't open to receiving our desires fall on deaf ears. Women think it is hard to achieve what they want. This kind of thinking prevents them from realizing their desires. No one ever said it had to be hard. If you choose to believe that, it will be. Start practicing letting yourself have what you want. That's all you really have to do - just let it in, let it in, let it in. There is no getting ready to let it in. Just let it in because it is time to let it in - because YOU say so!

When women get what they want by learning to let it in, they will benefit greatly and the world will be a better place to live. Women instinctively know how to live better than men. Even the bag lady on the street has more possessions around her than a homeless man. Women like to build nests and make things as comfortable and cozy as possible. Women need to trust that their desires will bring more good into the world. The simple fact that a woman has a desire for something is a good thing. And when she asks for it, she will get it, which is even better. She will become a happier, more fulfilled woman. This kind of woman will make the world a much nicer place to live.

Can you imagine happy women on every corner of the city nearest you? Everyone knows the affect of happy women. When women start to ask for what they want from the men in their life, the world will change and things which no man or woman could have dreamed, will begin to come their way. If you never ask for anything your dreams will never come true. The important thing to remember is never stop asking.

If you
really love
somebody,
you want
them to have
everything
they want...
including the
absence
of you.

Attributed to
Victor Baranco, Ph.D

Chapter 10

Men are More
Than Willing

Since the beginning of time it has been a man's goal to be the protector, provider and rescuer. This has always been their basic mode of operating. Men are the most gratified when acknowledged for the difference they make in a woman's life. Even today in the 21st century the fact still remains that men want to please women.

Men come one way, and that is willing. This is the most powerful realization I had about how man-woman relationships really work. Amazing things started to happen when I saw how ready and willing men really were. I realized a woman could have her tires changed without having to do it herself and have a man feel like a hero. Men would be willing to go to the market in the middle of the night, take her on the trip she's been wanting forever, rub her feet, and take out the garbage. They are willing to do just about anything as long as they are given the opportunity and asked in a nice way.

Men are dying to know what on earth they can do to make a woman happy. A man's biggest frustration is they don't how to do this. They would love the opportunity to put their talents, muscles, and abilities into action, but need a request. They are willing because they want to please and know if a woman isn't happy she won't be any fun.

A woman's biggest mistake is assuming men already know what they want. How on earth can a man know what a woman wants if she's not talking? The ball is in the woman's court. It is up to the woman to serve a man her request - to place her order. Men would be happy to produce for a woman anytime, especially if there is a win at the end for him. But making men wrong for not knowing what women want is totally ludicrous and ineffective. This kind of thinking will never get a woman what she wants.

Women can change things when they stop assuming and start communicating. Men have never known what really goes on with women and never will. All men know about women is what the last woman in their life taught them. Look around, you won't find many women mentoring men about women.

What would it cost a woman to let a man be her hero once in awhile? All it takes is a smile, a straight forward request, and some appreciation. Do these things and happier times are around the corner. Women don't understand that men get very little approval from women. In fact, whenever they do get a genuine smile and a thank you, it can change their whole day for the better. It makes them feel like they matter. Life becomes worth living. They made a difference and it doesn't get any better than that for a man. It sounds so simple, I know, but guess what? It is that simple.

♂♀

When women finally get the courage to ask for what they want, the first thing the man – producer will do, is doubt he can do it. He starts making grumbling noises that sound like resistance to her request. A man's grumbling is good news, not bad news. Men may say, "Oh no, we don't have the money, we don't have the time, we already did that, why do you need another one of those, etc." When this happens, women need to back off and give men the space to grumble. Women need to learn to play with men's grumbling and not think their request is being rejected.

For example, Jane asks Dick for a romantic evening. Dick grumbles about it. The grumbling is his way of expressing how much he values her. It's a sign he honors what she wants and how much he cares about her. When a woman asks a man for something he first considers doing it, then looks at all the reasons why he can't. He goes through his doubts and looks at where he might fail.

Too often woman think the grumbling means they are not going to get what they want. For too long women have been told NO. They've come to expect they can't have what they want.

A woman responds to a man's grumbling by thinking, "I knew I couldn't have what I want. I knew he didn't want to do this for me. I knew he'd come up with some excuse. I knew I'd have to do it myself", etc. etc.

Women become anxious when it feels like there's resistance to their desires, but in reality the grumble is a sign their request is being considered; nothing more. It means the man is working on his game plan to get her what she wants.

Women don't realize that when a man is grumbling he's contemplating the request and seeing whether he thinks he'll win or lose. He doesn't want to go forward if he thinks he'll fail. Men judge their ability to produce on the scale from failure to success. His grumbling gives him time to think before he actually commits. The breakdown happens if a woman becomes hooked by his grumbling and doubts his desire to produce for her. By getting hooked into his grumbling she adds her doubt to his doubt. In a man's mind two points of agreement equal reality. His confidence wanes which proves to him he can't produce what she wants. She castrates him and sinks her own ship. She doesn't get what she wants and he doesn't get to be the hero. Nobody wins!

How should women deal with a man's grumbling? Have fun with a man's grumbling and his resistance will go away. When a woman learns to play with his grumbling he will see her being fun instead of negative. When she doesn't doubt her man and truly believes she deserves it, her man will doubt his doubt. He will then be inspired to figure out how to produce what she wants. He will be in his glory. He will have a woman who believes in him!

Women need to help men win — they are not mind readers. The responsibility women have in getting their needs met starts with knowing that men cannot read their minds. Men can only win when they have clear instructions. The lack of clear instruction has been a major cause of much unnecessary suffering in relationships. If women would understand men are always poised for any opportunity to win, they would begin to finds ways to utilize this abundant flow of manpower.

How willing men are to please has been one of the biggest 'ah ha's' for women in my seminars over the years. Living life with the realization of how willing men are instead of how resistant they are, opens up a whole new world of possibilities for both sexes.

Here's the bottom line. When a woman is not talking, a man's only clue to what she wants comes from the look on her face. Men are not mind readers. They are not born knowing what women want. If women aren't telling them what they want, the only other source of data for them to use is her body language. Unfortunately, women cannot hide what they think or feel. It's always written on her face. One negative thought in a woman can transform a delightful afternoon into a complete and frightening nightmare. That's how helpless men feel when this is their only form of communication. They think, "Uh oh, we were just having a good time 30 seconds ago and now it looks like I'm in trouble and I didn't even say a word."

An example of this would be, Dick and Jane were out at a restaurant having good time. Jane went to the restroom and when she returned didn't look as happy as when she left. He said, "What's happening baby"? She said, "Oh nothing". The evening went downhill from there. Dick didn't know what happened. He believed that nothing was wrong because she said nothing was wrong. However, her face was not communicating this. Men get this kind of answer from women more than they care to.

If a woman hasn't been giving a man any clues on how he could win with her and he continues to feel like he's losing, he will feel like a failure. Men can only fail so much with a woman until they want to leave. However, men won't want to leave when they are winning and their woman is fun to be around.

Here's an example of what a man can be driven to do if a woman is constantly complaining. When I was living in Vancouver with my husband I had been complaining about everything. After about two weeks of this, he felt like he had the flu. He had no energy and felt physically ill. He asked me one day, "Is this what being castrated feels like?" I blew up in his face and we had the biggest fight ever. I stormed off in the car to the nearest Starbucks and 15 minutes later I called him to see how much damage I had done. I knew I had gotten really ugly with him and I knew deep down he was right.

He told me he had called a cab and they were coming to take him to the airport. He had a one- way ticket to Miami and was going to visit his best friend, Mike. I freaked out and tried to back pedal. I tried to apologize. I told him I didn't really mean everything I said. He said, "I'm sorry baby but I'm done". I'm thinking, 'holy moly it's over'! I drove 90 miles an hour back to the house with my relationship flashing before my eyes. I'm thinking, 'This can't be happening', but it was the first time he'd hung up on me and I knew he was serious. I got home and came flying through the door to see suitcases everywhere. I raced to the bedroom and flung open the door where I found him lying on the bed with his finger pointing at me saying, "Gotcha!"

He had set me up perfectly to think he was leaving. All I could do at that moment was beat on his chest and yell, "How could you do this to me?" I realized how much he really loved me to take the time to pull this off. I'd hit bottom in my relationship with him, so the only direction to go was up. At this point the only thing left to do was get happy. I started to have a good time and never got that ugly again. I had pushed him all the way to wanting to leave me. From this point on our relationship turned around forever. I knew all I had to do was tell him what I wanted. I didn't need to do anymore complaining.

All it takes for a man to want to leave is for him to go off to the 7-11 one night and run into a woman who asks nicely for something that she wants. She becomes the new opportunity to produce for, a friendly woman who appreciates him. That's how easy an affair can start. Men are attracted to other women when they are not appreciated at home.

Men everywhere are looking for an opportunity to be a hero. Look out ladies! If you don't give your man the opportunity to be your hero some other woman will. Men have to be heroes. Their very existence depends on having something to do where they succeed at the end. The more fun and attractive the cycle is, the more they will do it. I continue to express these points as simply as I can. This is not rocket science. It's as simple as women telling men what they want with a smile on their face and appreciation in their heart.

Relationship
requires
viewing oneself
through
all of
another's
perceptions.

Attributed to
Victor Baranco, Ph.D

Chapter 11

Are You Talkin' To Me?!

Achieving effortless and fulfilling communication with the opposite sex is not as difficult as it appears. However, to have communication flow, we need to accept and embrace our differences. Once we begin celebrating our differences instead of resisting them, we will quickly find ourselves in a new dance, treating each other as we would like to be treated, with honor and respect.

This is critical to relationships because being connected is all about communication. The only thing that separates us is what we are not willing to share. When we begin to hold our circumstances as opportunities to be more connected, we will be heading down the right track.

Women don't realize what happens when they share what they *don't* want with their man. They think they are communicating what they want by telling a man what they *don't* want. All he knows is she's not happy and he doesn't know what to do to win. Women don't see that if you share your *don'ts* with a man it doesn't give him any avenue to produce what you 'do' want. This is one of the disastrous ways women communicate with men which produces a huge negative effect.

When men have no direction from a woman they feel useless with no way to win. It would be a very smart move for women to tell men exactly what they want. This would inspire men simply because it would give them a direction and another opportunity to win. All a man wants to know is that he can win with whatever cycle he starts.

Women talk in circles and men want the bottom line. Women speak *womanese* and men speak *manese*. Men and women speak different languages. Women want to be felt. When they are talking in a group they want to feel each other's energy. Imagine a whole gaggle of girls standing around talking. They all talk at the same time, going warp speed, and they are tracking everything that's being said. It's not a difficult thing for women to do. It's actually quite enlivening and pleasurable for women. This, however, would be frightening for men. They cannot maintain this speed, nor do they care to. It's very frustrating for them.

Men just want to know the bottom line because they want to produce. They are driven by production. When a group of men are talking only one will speak at a time. Each man will wait until the next one is done before they add their two bits. This would be much too slow for women. This is why a conversation is more fun when there are two women and a man. The two women keep the juice going, and the man can tune in or out whenever he wants. It doesn't matter to the women if he checks out, because they have each other to relate with. Two women enjoy having a man around when they are talking as long as he doesn't ruin their fun.

If a woman wants to communicate with a man she has to slow it way down and be more logical in her speaking, otherwise she will lose him. Men only have the capacity to listen to women for a certain amount of time.

♂♀

Good communication requires accepting who people are. People are the way they are and that's all there is to it. Women can spend their whole lives trying to make men different or can realize what a perfect compliment they can be. Men are exactly perfect the way they are; so are women. Not accepting our differences in any way produces absolutely nothing, except more separation.

Men have built-in barometers. Even though they may not know what is going on with a woman, they can feel when she's angry. They can feel her anger even when she says there's nothing wrong. You can't fool men in this department. They know the difference between yuck and yum and are more sensitive than women give them credit for. The one thing women need to know for sure is *men do not improve with abuse*. The more upset and angry women become about a man's behavior, the further away men take themselves.

It would be smart if men and women would allow for the fact that they are going to have conflict in relating. Sometimes fights are almost as good as sex. Anger has 11 of the 14 physical attributes of being sexually aroused. Fighting actually discharges the same energy that sex discharges. If we were to accept fighting as necessary to the growth of the relationship, the fight could be over and the love would begin.

It's okay, even admirable, to acknowledge in the middle of a fight that you don't know it all - that you could be wrong. Do you want to be right or do you want to be connected? Getting out of your mind and getting into the present moment would help you to have a different outlook on the situation.

Life always looks different when you *Be Here Now*. The saying "This too shall pass," is always good to remember in the middle of a mess.

There have been many men who think because they have more muscle than women, they can somehow control women by getting angry. Here is a word of caution to all men who attempt this - don't go there. It is an instant formula for disaster.

Here's an example. Carol wasn't being heard. Bob would often come home angry as a result of his stressful day. He would take it out on Carol. This would upset her, however, she would suppress herself verbally. Her anger would come out in other ways. She'd ruin his clothes in the washer, wouldn't have his favorite foods in the fridge, and she even put a dent in his luxury car. This is the tip of the iceberg of what a woman can do when she is angry. Women are much too powerful for men to express their unwarranted anger towards them.

Men have no idea how much anger women have. They don't realize women feel all the atrocities currently happening to their sisters around the world. Every time women are slighted in any way, whether on TV, newspapers, magazines, or in conversations, women feel it. Women are angry that the world is still treating their sisters in such unforgivable ways. Men only see the tip of the iceberg of a woman's anger. There is nothing more intimidating to a man than an angry woman.

Women are way too powerful to be expressing themselves in a negative way. They have too much of an effect on those around them. The world cannot afford to treat the female population with anything other than respect, if it is ever going to receive the full benefit of feminine energy.

♂♀

When men and women are fighting about something there's always someone who is not being heard. If you give up your need to be right it will open up the space to be heard. If you are wrong you can always be forgiven. The first person to realize they are in a situation that is spiraling downward is the person who can take it in another direction. All it takes is one person having the goal of staying connected and any disagreement can be over in a minute. Simply agree to disagree. Being committed to your anger instead of your connection ruins many relationships. Give up being right and love will follow.

People feel safe with each other when they know they are not being judged. We all want to feel totally accepted for who we are and what we do. Unfortunately, we have to accept ourselves first before we can accept others. We usually blame others for things we don't like about ourselves. What separates us from another is what we judge and withhold.

When you know everyone is doing the best they can, it would be smart to put yourself in the same boat. This awareness will have a huge impact on reducing the negative drama in your life. If you choose to be responsible for how you experience your life, you no longer have to be victimized by anyone or anything. You can observe what's so about a situation and simply take appropriate action.

The cleanest way to communicate with another is to take responsibility for what you are feeling by speaking from the place of, 'I feel', not 'You made me feel'. 'You made me feel' makes the other person feels like they are being accused. The conversation becomes defensive and both sides end up losing. Shift from, "You made me crazy when you did that", to "I felt crazed when that happened". It's a much more friendly way of saying what you need to say which won't cause the other person to be defensive.

We need to remember that all our mistakes are learning opportunities. It's simple. The dance of life changes every day. We need to allow our relationships to change too. Communication doesn't have to be difficult if you stay in present time. After all, life is only happening right now. One of our biggest mistakes is thinking life is happening tomorrow or next week.

We miss the point in our communications if we think something or someone should be different than they are. Life is only happening right now and there are no mistakes. Now is never wrong!

There are no final solutions to anything. Why not figure out how to enjoy yourself along the way? If your life is about getting to some goal, you are missing the opportunity of truly being with another. It's not about getting to some illusive goal. It's about, "Are you having fun NOW?"

If you can't find perfection in the moment most likely you are judging and resisting it. This is a waste of precious time and energy. If you want to stop judging simply decide to stop doing it. Stop talking about the negative, stop thinking about it, and it will cease to exist. Stop judging and joy will be yours in a heartbeat.

Appetite
is the
Flame
of
Life.

Attributed to
Victor Baranco, Ph.D

Chapter 12

Guess Who Wins?

A very smart man once said, "If we don't figure out what women want, they will torture us and make our life miserable." No truer words were ever spoken. It's very clear the world is in better shape where women are having their needs met. If they are having their needs met, they are happy, and every man will tell you a happy woman is a joy to be around.

A woman can have everything she wants from a man. At the same time, she can also have him be thrilled about giving her what she wants. Most women don't believe this; they don't think men get that much gratification from producing for them. The truth is, men love it when women get what they want. When she's satisfied and gratified, it's written all over her face. If he had something to do with making her happy, he will feel like a winner. And we all know men are addicted to winning.

One of the reasons women have a hard time receiving from men is because they know they haven't been very nice to them. Women, on some level, don't feel they deserve such kindness. Relationships will not achieve the level of satisfaction possible until women begin to receive what men are willing to produce for them.

In order for a woman to get what she wants, she must learn these powerful steps to communicate her desires. The first step is to *get a man's attention in an attractive way*. In order to get a man's attention, a woman has to say something that will make him feel he is winning. She needs to acknowledge him by approving of something he's already done. It has to be genuine; something that is true for her. You can't fool men. If it isn't genuine, it will feel like manipulation. If she can't find anything she approves of, she may be with the wrong man. When a man feels a woman's sincere acknowledgement and approval, he will automatically feel like a winner. He will be calm, comfortable and confident, which is rare for a man. This will capture his attention. He will be open to listen for her next desire.

The second step is to *ask for what you want*. Make sure your heart is open and be present to how fortunate you are to have a man willing to listen to what you want. Use the words, "You know what I'd love? I would love it if we could…." and then fill in what you want. Men love to hear what women love, because if they know you love it, it means you would be happy to get it. Be proud of what you want. Know you deserve it, and see him happily producing for you. Remember, men are always looking for ways to make women happy. This is their one and only goal with women.

The third step is to *express your appreciation and gratitude*. This could be the most important step of all. A woman needs to tell her man how much she appreciates any move he makes toward her desire. Women simply need to give men approval. The way to a man's heart is to approve of him. It doesn't cost her anything to offer appreciation. She won't get what she wants if she leaves out this last step. Only after expressing her gratitude for something he's done will there space to start the three steps over again.

These steps are also very effective in educating a man about what you want sexually. When a man alters the direction he's going because of your request, make sure you acknowledge the change right away with a pleasurable sigh, a moan, or appreciative words.

A man is more than willing to play with you as long as you use the three steps every time. Find something about him that you can approve of. Ask in a nice way for what you want. And acknowledge him for whatever he's doing toward your goal. You can't leave out the first step or the third step, otherwise, he won't feel appreciated for what he has done. It will feel like manipulation. If women would adopt an attitude of gratitude for everything men do for them, there would be many happy men around.

One thing to know about men is they love to be acknowledged for their production, not their looks. It makes them uneasy when too much attention is put on their physical appearance. This is unlike women who love as many compliments as they can get, especially about their appearance.

Men love to know exactly what women want. If a woman is too vague, it robs a man of the opportunity to hit a home run for her. I once took my partner to a special European lingerie store when we were living in Oxford, England. The purpose was to show him the different types of lingerie that were special to me. I let him know ahead of time this was not a buying trip, just an information trip. I cruised through everything in the store and showed him exactly what I liked and why I liked it. There were a dozen, or so, items I pulled off the rack and went crazy over. He clearly saw what he could do to win big with me.

I moved back to Vancouver three weeks before my partner did. When I went to pick him up at the airport, he walked off the plane with only two things in his hands; two bags stuffed to the gills with all the lingerie I'd gone wild over in Oxford. He bought every item I loved. He was my total hero and hit the jackpot of appreciation from me for many moons.

♂ ♀

We left the store without buying anything. I was happy to have the opportunity to show him what I loved. It was very special to me that he took the time to find out what made me happy. And he felt more confident because he had some new ideas of how he could be my hero when the time was right.

Women don't want to be responsible for training a man. It looks like an impossible task to them. However, if women are willing to educate men to their needs and wants, there is nothing they couldn't have. All women have to do is make it fun and there's not much men won't do for them.

When a woman doubts a man's ability, she removes his desire to produce for her. Trust that your man is capable and willing to give you whatever you want. Don't hold out on the good times while you are waiting for him to produce what you asked him for. A man knows if a woman is not happy with what she has now, she won't be happy in the future either. When a woman is unwilling to enjoy her life now, it doesn't inspire a man to produce anything for her. It's a losing proposition. Women must ask for what they want, then savor the waiting and enjoy the ride. Your ship will come in over a non-anxious sea.

Women don't just want a new red dress. If they say that's all they want, they have ordered short. They want shoes and a purse to match. Jewelry would be good too, and then, of course, something for the man to wear to compliment her outfit. A way women castrate men is to order short. Too often, a woman looks at how much money a man has and then decides what she can and can't have. It's really okay to admit you want it all. And just for the record, women don't want it later, they want it now, if at all possible. Men can produce without money. What a woman wants should not be dependant on how much money is available. Women need to be open to the creative ways men can produce. Men can be very creative, especially when they know it will result in a happy woman.

Women need to know what they want. The more they exercise their 'desire' muscle, the easier it becomes. Men find it very attractive when they meet women who know what they want and are committed to getting it, no matter what.

The more specific you are, the more he gets to be your hero. Nothing is worse for a man than to buy a woman something and have her be disappointed. He can just look at the woman's face and know he has failed. When women are out and about in the world with their man, and see their favorite flowers, it would be smart for her to say, "Ooooh, I love tulips, especially the pale pink ones. These are my favorite kind." Saying what you love with enthusiasm will be immediately logged on to his memory file called, "How To Win Buying Flowers for My Honey."

Always look for opportunities to educate men. Whether it's jewelry, your favorite watch, the kind of wine you like best, the type of materials you like for clothes, lingerie, etc. When I'm with my man and see a couple being sexy and having fun with each other, I simply say, "Hmmmm, love that - look at them - that looks yummy!" I'm always giving him information about what would make me happy.

You must first perceive in your mind what you want before you can receive it. We have to look deep inside ourselves to know what we want in every area of life. Ask, ask, ask and a world of joy awaits you. Whether you ask verbally to the world, or quietly to yourself, the more you ask for what you want, the more likely it will manifest. Write a list of everything you want, date it, and put it on your fridge. You will be amazed how quickly the items will start to show up, especially if you read it every day and see yourself having it. If a woman knows she will get what she wants, no matter where it comes from, she has begun the process of achieving all her dreams.

The physical universe wants to deliver everything you want. You simply need to get out of your own way. The only thing in the way of receiving everything you want is the unloving thoughts you have. Unloving thoughts produce a vibration that literally push away what you ask for.

Choose loving thoughts over fearful ones. Find ways to be grateful for everything in your life and more will come your way. Take a look around and find 10 things you love. Then find another 10. The more you exercise the 'grateful' muscle, the easier it is to fill every moment with the goodness of life. Before falling asleep acknowledge and appreciate all the good experiences from your day. You will sleep in a zone that is very nourishing to your soul.

Love begets love, fear begets fear, and gratitude gets you everything your heart desires. We have all adopted our own particular attitude about life. Change yours to an attitude of gratitude and watch how fast the doors of manifestation fly open, filling your life with joy and abundance.

Let your feminine charm and intuition be your guide. To be born a woman in these times is very special. Women have so much of an opportunity to contribute to the world by simply being a woman. All they have to do is enjoy life, have fun in the moment, and be charming and grateful for how good their lives are. An army of men will show up at their door to see how they can make it even better.

Women need to appreciate, approve and acknowledge the men in their lives. This will always be attractive to men. Women do know how to do this. They also know when they are being unattractive. Being attractive, by being generous with their approval, is what they did to get a man in the first place. It is what it takes to keep a man by her side forever. This insight is a golden nugget worth much more than the price of this book.

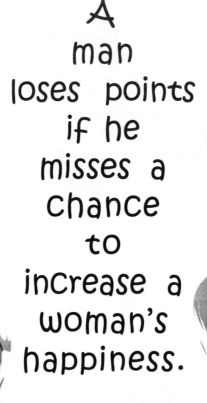

A
man
loses points
if he
misses a
chance
to
increase a
woman's
happiness.

Attributed to
Victor Baranco, Ph.D

Chapter 13

What Women Do 24/7

Women are driven by a need to fulfill their life mission even if they haven't defined it. On some subconscious level a woman knows she can only be with a man who will give her the space she needs to achieve her goals. When women are interested in having a life partner, it is vital for her to find a man who 'fits the bill'. There is a quiet accounting that occurs '24/7' whenever a woman relates with a man. Women notice everything a man does and then evaluates how they feel about him.

Men fall in love and women make deals. Men think being in love is the basis for being married. Women know the deal has to be right or she can't afford to fall in love with him.

A woman feels loved and honored by a man when he supports who she is and everything she wants to be. She needs to be free to be herself. This is the deal that has to be right. She knows the man who truly loves her will inspire her to stretch to new possibilities. When she feels squashed or suppressed in any way, it feels like control, not love. True love grants her the freedom to be fully engaged in her life path. When a man can offer his love this way, it becomes a done deal for a woman.

Women evaluate everything about a man and are constantly giving him ✔ s and Xs. They don't miss a thing; they check everything out. They naturally observe and grade everything that is going on as a form of quality control for a pleasurable life. They either approve of whatever a man is doing by giving him a check ✔ or disapprove of him and give him Xs on his balance sheet. If a woman grades him with too many Xs she will have to move on. She will not surrender to such a man because, in her heart, she knows he doesn't fit the bill. His actions won't support what she wants.

Women are looking for men who have lots of ✔ s. Women would love to be able to approve of everything about a man. This would give him lots of ✔ s which would be an answer to her prayers.

However, we are dealing with a world of men who don't realize how some of their behaviors affect women. Some men are not as awake as women would like them to be. Women know shortly after meeting a man whether or not he will require a lot of work. Many women are unwilling to be care givers for men and their baggage. If women find that men are too much work and get too many Xs, the balance sheet will be in the red. And red is a big stop sign.

Men, on the other hand, are hungry to fall in love. It inspires their production. Falling in love is easy for a man. It's like falling off a log, and they are usually unaware when this happens. All they know is, a woman has her full attention on him in an attractive way. It looks and feels like good times are here. Being in love inspires a man to produce beyond what he thought he could. Men love this feeling more than anything. There's nothing more powerful for a man's production than falling in love with a woman who approves of him. Something big happens for a man when he falls in love. You often see ads in newspapers,

"Getting married - Must sell '57 Chevy with over 20,000 hours invested", which reflects his willingness to give up things that mean a lot to him.   ♂♀

It has to feel safe for a woman to fall in love. Safe is a word that means everything to a woman. This is very important for her, because if it feels unsafe, she will end up operating out of fear, instead of love. She has to keep her guard up, which will prevent her from falling in love.

The more ✔ s a man gets, the safer the woman feels. When you ask a man what 'safe' means, they usually don't have a clue. Women feel safe when they have a man they can give lots of ✔ s to. Women easily approve of a man when he is doing and saying all the right things. There are many universal issues that show up for all women, one of which is the need to feel respected and taken seriously by men.

Men get ✔ s when they arrive on time, call if they are going to be late, remember special occasions, tell her how beautiful she looks, have a clean car, treat waiters with respect, are interested in her family and friends, buy good bottles of wine, bring flowers for no reason, keep their fingernails well manicured, buy small gifts that have special meaning, call up after a date to say how much fun they had, send fun and sexy e-mails, call just to see how she's doing, appreciate how much she loves her pets, and take charge at a busy restaurant to make sure they have good service. Also when they hold her when she's feeling blue, give her long, slow, yummy kisses, and shoulder rubs. They get ✔ s when they are considerate drivers, let her pick the movies, put attention on her at parties, live in an environment that is conscious, open doors for her and assist her out of a car. When they have great music to listen to for their car and the bedroom, when they return calls that she makes to them in a timely manner and when they give her big warm hugs every time they see her, these will also bring big ✔ s.

97

One thing women must have is a man of his word. He has to be trustworthy. Women need to know they can count on a man to do what he says. Nothing drives a woman crazy, faster than a man without integrity; it won't feel safe to her. Her world will become uncertain and she will have a difficult time being present. She will become obsessed with wondering what he may do next. All her creative energy will shift to worrying. This becomes a nightmare for her and will inevitably lead to a big X.

The ultimate X is any kind of abuse - physical, verbal, emotional or psychological. One incident of physical abuse and a man is out! Women must honor themselves enough to realize there is absolutely no excuse, plain and simple. Any kind of abuse from a man, no matter what form, is inexcusable. Women need to know, if a man does it once, he'll do it again; it's a red flag! They should take heed because people don't change their basic mode of operating. If the woman feels abused and degraded in anyway, she is. She need not doubt herself. And it is NOT her job to change him. She must move on. Too many women become the caregivers and think they can change men. It will never happen.

The more ✔ s a man gets the more of his woman he gets to experience. Men love to play games because somebody is always winning. The man-woman game can be one of the most enjoyable games to play. For a man, a great way to play, would be to see how many ✔ s he could get from his woman. One thing is for sure, every time he gets a ✔ from her, it will be a positive experience. The woman will be happy and will let down her guard to show other fun sides of herself.

There's a world of different women inside of every woman. Men don't realize if they acquired nothing but ✔ s from a woman, she would trust him enough to relax and show him all her buttons, levers and dials, that up until now, were not safe to reveal. There are many different aspects to every woman. If men were safe for women, they would rarely think about the grass being greener over yonder hill. A safe man would allow a woman to express all of the amazing, playful, and wonderful creatures that she knows she is. The grass will be green enough to keep him entertained and content for a long time.

When men create a safe space for women, there's nothing women won't do for them. Women are natural care givers and would like to see everybody have what they want. If a man gives a woman the 'inch' she needs to feel safe, she will give him a 'mile'. She will add her energy, love and support to anything he wants to do. Everyone knows behind every great man is a powerful woman. Actually, behind every great man is a woman who is happy because she feels safe with her man. Only when a woman feels safe will a man get her full and complete endorsement.

Both men and women are judging and evaluating how they make each other feel all the time. It's no secret we are both doing this on some level. If men would have more fun with what's important to a woman, they would be assured of having their needs met as well. That's the way the man-woman game works. Make the woman happy first and the man will be happy next. It can be instantaneous. Giving to a woman for the pure enjoyment of it will insure big a's for a man every time. It's actually possible to have fun with the man-woman game.

The greatest gift a man can give a woman is to listen to her and trust that what she says is what she means. Then, if it feels good, offer total support to whatever she wants. Most women have not experienced being truly heard by men. Women want men to know that when a man is fully behind her, she will steer the relationship in a direction where both of you win every time. If men are going to play the man-woman game, the sanest way to play is with a big YES!

Niceness comes from strength; meanness comes from weakness.

Attributed to
Victor Baranco, Ph.D

Chapter 14

Forgive Women for They Know Not What They Do

One of the major reasons there is so much upset and confusion in man-woman relationships is because women relate with men as if men understand a woman's language. Many times she will unknowingly cut him to the bone with her words. She assumes she is getting through to him in a clear manner, and doesn't realize the problem she's actually creating. Women castrate men in ways they are not aware of. Their castrating actions make men feel less of a man.

When I ask men what it's like for them to be with women in general, they say they 're on edge much of the time. They're waiting for the next time they do something wrong. Women let men know, in many ways, when they are not happy with them. Women have a hard time believing that their simple comments can produce such negative effects on men. Men feel like they get hit from all angles.

Castration happens in many ways. *Frontal castration* is when a woman complains, straight out, that a man has done something wrong. It's one of the kindest forms of castration because he knows where it came from. When a woman is clearly not pleased by what she sees or what he's done, she will come straight out and say so. "That was a terrible haircut she gave you" or, "Don't you ever wash your car?" or, "Did YOU pick that shirt out?" or, "You like your cologne, eh?" or, "It sounds like you job is going nowhere." This may be blatant, but it's actually a form of castration that a man can swallow more easily. It's direct and to the point.

Beartrapping castration happens when a woman asks a man for help with her problem, then continues to change some aspect of it. She never lets him win, and never gives him any acknowledgment for his efforts. She continues to tell him why it can't be fixed over and over again disregarding his current solution. She continues to add new information. The man tries to follow her lead again, but she won't acknowledge his efforts or let him win. He continues to try to fix something for her, but she never approves of anything he does. This goes on and on until it is clear to the man there is no way to win. He becomes exasperated, and quickly recognizes it is a lose-lose situation. He throws his hands up and says, "Do it yourself!"

Women don't realize how devastating this is to a man's spirit. All a man wants is for her be happy with everything in her world. When a woman doesn't let him fix the problem she's asked him to fix, he will feel like a complete failure. It feels bad to a man when his ability to produce is wasted.

There's another way women castrate men and make then feel bad. It's called *Blindspot castration*. In this form, one minute men think they are winning and have produced a home run for their woman, and the next minute they feel bad because she made a negative comment that took his win away. The man doesn't catch it when she says the negative comment, because he's been blindsided with the original compliment. His ego got fluffed up and he missed the second thing she said. For example, after a great dinner and evening out a woman says, "Gosh that was a fabulous restaurant and a totally delicious meal." The man thinks he's winning until she says, "Too bad the service sucked." Women think these 'light' comments don't really bother a man. They have no idea how earth shattering this can be.

Women constantly doubt many aspects of their own lives. They doubt their attractiveness, their intelligence, their ability, and their body, just to name few. The root cause for women to doubt themselves is a lack of self-esteem. When men feel a woman's doubt, it makes them feel powerless. Men see how powerful women are and don't understand why they doubt themselves. For example, it feels terrible when a man says something nice to a woman and she rejects his compliment. He feels stupid and it's painful because he feels dismissed. Also, when a man goes to open a door for a woman and she looks right past him, she is saying 'I don't need you'. This hurts a man's ego.

Men are always responding to women. They don't have a choice whether they respond, but they do have a choice how they respond. A simple sigh, gesture or closed body language from an unhappy woman is all it takes to make a man feel bad. Women can devastate men in very subtle ways. Men may not know what on earth is going on with women at any particular time, but they have a unique sensitivity, a built in barometer. They know the difference between yuck and yum, and will naturally go toward yum.

My friend, Vince, once caught me being mean shortly after we starting dating. I was castrating him in some way. He let me know that he felt the attack and would catch it in the future too. He insisted I play clean with him. He let me know he was on my team. He did not return my mean behavior, but simply gave me feedback as to how it felt to him. It's hard for some men to do this, especially if they haven't experienced women who will cop to how mean they can be.

Women resist the fact that men are accurate responders. Men are the kind of creatures who wake up in the morning and look forward to having a great productive day. On the other hand, a woman can wake-up in the morning, and will find a way to ruin his day, if she is still upset with him. Women have been known to castrate and sabotage men until they are heard. Men should remember to never reward a woman's bad behavior. If she does something really ugly, don't send her flowers.

When a woman does emotional terrorism on a man, and he lets it go, it will come back to bite him . The message he missed was, "I want you to pay attention to me. I have an issue I am trying to deal with, and I need you to help me resolve it." Women do this kind of behavior because they are desperate to be heard. They feel a part of them dies every time they don't get heard.

If a man feels bad, the truth is, a woman intended him to feel this way. The statement, 'true intention is demonstrated by attainment' is a powerful truth. Women need to realize the state their relationship is in, is how they intended it to be, whether they are conscious of this or not. If the man is happy, she intended him to be happy. If he's not happy, that's also what she intended.

When a woman is willing to take responsibility for the effect she has on a man, she will have much more control over steering the relationship in the direction she wants.

If a man lets a woman get away with mean behavior, she won't respect him. A woman wants to respect her man first and foremost. No respect equals no relationship. It's not a woman's nature to be mean, she simply gets caught up in her self-created drama. If a man turns away from a woman's wrath, she knows he is weak. She knows she can control and castrate him any time she wants. This kind of man is not attractive to a woman because she knows he will not make her accountable for future unloving behavior. If he lets her get away with this, she won't be able to move toward more love in her life. Women want to play it straight with men and need gentle reminders for them to lighten up and control less.

Men need to give women a reality check when it hurts. What women want is a new age John Wayne. They want a manly man, who's tough, but sensitive, at the same time. When a woman says something that hurts, a man needs to say OUCH! He has to get a woman's attention from a gentle place. A woman needs a man to communicate from his heart, not from his need to be right about how wrong she is. He will never get her to change her behavior, unless the reality he gives her is from his heart.

Men owe it to women to tell them their emotional truth. He owes her the truth about how it feels to him. Men always want to leave a relationship if it's too painful. If he feels like a loser around her, he should tell her so. He should not say that she's doing it to him, but can ask, "Are you all right? Did I miss something?" That's always a good thing to ask, because he probably did miss something.

If you ask a man what happened to their relationship and why it ended, most of them say they think they're at fault; not responsible, but at fault. Somehow, they did it wrong.

What men end up with is the notion they are the reason why it didn't work. It's not a safe world for men, but they are ready to pop for a woman any time it is safe.

The most loving thing a woman can do, is give her man the true picture of what is going on with her. A woman has to be willing to educate him and must be responsible for how she does it. If she comes across needing to be right, instead of wanting to let him know how he can win with her, nobody wins. Men are ready and willing to learn. They learn best when women are in touch with just how willing they are.

It's not so much what a woman says, it's how she says it. Have you ever heard a woman say, "All I said was….", wondering why her man is so upset with her? That's because it's not what a woman says, it's how she says it. It's the intonation in her voice. It's whether she intends to have the man feel bad or understand her communication. Women have to be rigorous in their speaking. Men may not understand what is going on with women, but they do know the difference between something that feels good and something that feels bad.

When women understand their true power and how it affects men, they will have more compassion for men. Once women realize how much of a partner men can be, they will begin to look at them in a whole new way. They will look around and see all the things men do in the world to make it a better place to live. Being born a man is very different than being born a woman. Men are mostly at the mercy of a woman's power. They know that women can out think, out market, out plan, and out maneuver them. They are just trying to find some way to play with women, so they can make it through the day and avoid getting beaten up.

Women need to stop making men wrong if they are ever going to have peace on earth. Men are not wrong, just uninformed about the smarter half, not the better half, of the planet. Is it their fault? No, it's just the way it is. Women don't see that men are never going to improve in the ways women want, unless they have more compassion and understanding for them. The sooner women learn to take these gentle men under their wing, and teach them instead of torment them, the sooner they will have men the way they want them. They will become confident, sexy and trustworthy men.

The ability
to enjoy
where you are
offers
enjoyment
wherever
you go.

Attributed to
Victor Baranco, Ph.D

Chapter 15

Straight Talk about the 'C' Word

For many people, the word commitment brings up much anxiety. It brings up worry, apprehension, angst and fear. We hear the word commitment and our heart skip a beat. It can trigger confusion and stressful memories of moments in our lives that didn't turn out the way we had hoped. It's a sad state of affairs when such a powerful word elicits such fear and trepidation. What if we commit, and it turns out to be a nightmare? Fortunately, there are no mistakes. To be truly committed to someone or something can be a very powerful and life altering experience. Being committed to something outside of yourself is a way to bring a whole new energy to what you are doing. It brings lightness and peace of mind to your relationships.

Women are mystified why so many men have so much charge on the subject of commitment. Most women think men don't want to commit. The opposite is true, even though it looks like they get intimidated by the whole conversation. Being committed and in love inspires a man to deliver his optimum production.

Women usually want a commitment from men early on in the relationship. They think a commitment will insure that the man won't leave when the going gets rough. They know there will be times when things won't flow so smoothly. Women don't realize men would love to commit, but not to something that won't be fun.

A man would love to love a woman who wants and appreciates everything about him and all that he does for her. They want to commit to women who feel good about being women. This makes them feel good.

A man's biggest fear about commitment is that he will lose the thing he cherishes most - his freedom. He thinks a woman will take over his life and usurp all his time and attention. This wouldn't be such a bad thing, if all his time and attention on her produced more fun. Men are realistic enough to know this will not be the case. Men know when they commit to a woman they are taking on the good, the bad and the ugly.

Commitment allows a man the opportunity to produce on a grand scale. Producing on this level makes a man feel great. Men are not interested in committing to an unhappy woman. They steer away from women who are miserable and committed to their drama. They are smart enough to know they won't be able to fix her problems, especially if she's committed to telling her victim story over and over. It would be a hopeless undertaking. It can make him feel sick to his stomach when his woman is suffering. He doesn't want to be around this. The bottom line is - men are repelled by unhappy women.

It's very simple to operate a man to have him commit. Women simply need to remember that men want to win, not just sometimes, all the time. Men want to commit to someone that is fun. If they are winning and feel like they make a difference in their woman's life, they will go for it with gusto and stick around forever. It's so simple. All women have to do is be happy and appreciative and a man will have no problem with the "C" word. Men have one goal - to win with women. A happy woman is their greatest win. He can live a good life without a lot of money if he has a happy woman.

A man has a goal to make his woman happy for the rest of her life. If she has a bad hair day and is losing about it, even though it has nothing to do with him, he will take it on like he was responsible for producing hers terrible day. This is the job a man gives himself, to fix everything that is broken. When a woman looks broken, they can't imagine why anyone would want to live this way, so they'll try to fix it.

His woman is the biggest opportunity for him to be a hero. If she's not happy he loses, especially if he doesn't express himself. That's why men pick up sports. It's a place where they can win. They can lose anytime in the man-woman game. However, in man and his muse, he will always have the opportunity to win; to play his guitar better. His guitar will never judge him or dump him if he misses a chord.

The best life a man will ever have is determined by how willing his woman is to enjoy herself. Since all men do is respond to women, if she is committed to living a life less than wonderful, he won't have a chance of having his life be any better as long as he is with her.

Women sometimes live in a space called the 'hagomatic' mode. If she has gone too long without the quality attention she needs, she can be a nightmare to deal with. She's like a persnickety cat. If he's not careful, he will get scratched. If a man gets scratched too often, it's sometimes easier for him to check out early, than to live to for any length with a 'hagomatic'.

Women are in denial about the power they have, and how much they run every aspect of a relationship. A man has a hard time committing to a woman who doesn't know her own power or is in denial about it. Men know women are the ones who really wear the pants. If a woman isn't responsible for her power, it leaves too many ways for men to fail. At some point, she is bound make him the enemy, and will decide she is once again the victim. Women always end up being the victim when they don't own their power. When they owns their power, they know how to get what they want, and never have to be victimized. When a woman own her power, it's safe for a man to get behind her vision.

Men respond best to straight talk from a woman. Nothing is more refreshing for a man, than a woman who is up front and straight about who she is and what she wants. Men love to know where a woman stands at all times. They like to be in some semblance of control. When women are honest, straight forward and to the point, men feel safe. They can trust this kind of woman. She is a breath of fresh air and a relief for them to relate with.

Men know that women run the show more than women realize. Men don't like to admit this, but they know it's the truth. The fastest way to more fun in life is for women to realize the ball is in their court. It's always been in their court. Until now this truth has never been revealed or acknowledged.

For women to realize they run the show might be frightening at first. However, once they get over the shock and learn to embrace this, it will set them free. As long as women resist they are in charge, they will remain with the old school of thinking, and the divorce rate will continue to rise.

This is not about women controlling men. It's about acknowledging the perfect balance that's available when men and women tell the truth about the way it is. When we were born, we were wrapped in either a blue blanket or a pink one. From the very beginning our differences were defined.

A man is empowered when a woman realizes how much of an affect she has on him. When a woman gives herself permission to have fun with this power, she will be a lot less intimidating. She will see instant changes in her relationship with men. A smart woman will use this power wisely. She will use it to fulfill both their needs.

Women are not interested in controlling men. They want to empower them to be more manly. They have the ability to use their feminine power positively in every interaction with men. A woman is in her true power when she is grateful for her role in the relationship. It will become easy to steer the relationship in a direction where they both win.

It's this easy. If a woman wants a man to commit, all she needs to do is make sure he is winning. If she is having fun and enjoying her life, her man is winning and will want to stay around. As she continues to enjoy her life day after day, lo and behold, the man will still want be around. He's not going to leave as long as she is enjoying herself. It's a simple fact. Enjoy the moment and a man will stay forever. Men are happy to commit to anything or anyone who is fun. This point cannot be said enough – women who are happy equal men who stick around.

Fun is what makes the world go round. People love to have fun. Everything people do is to have fun either now or later. They don't do things to intentionally bring themselves miserable lives. When you decide to have fun in the moment you automatically become a more enjoyable person to be around. Only then will you begin to attract more lighthearted people into your life.

Getting to 'I Do' is as easy as having fun. Think about when couples say "I Do". They get together. It is fun and full of love, which makes it easy to tie the knot. If people think being married for the rest of their lives is not going to be any fun, they would never consider it. If you make it your goal in life to have fun, getting to 'I Do' will be a piece of cake - wedding cake!

No one wants to commit to a future that may turn out to be a bad one. A woman has a huge ability to impact the direction the relationship will go. If she commits to have each day be the best it can be, the chances of having the relationship of her dreams will be greatly improved. How about having each day and date being good, rather than trying to work out the rest of your life in one evening. Let go of the future, have a good time now.

People commit to many things like their job, their exercise, their lawn care, and their house cleaning. Are they having any fun? No, not much! If people would commit to fun in everything they do, no matter what, their experience of living would totally transform. They would wake up every day with nothing but opportunities for more fun. We can choose to bring fun into what we are doing or we can continue in the direction we've been going. It's always a choice.

One thing is for sure. When women are committed to fun, they glow and sparkle, and catch the attention of every man around. Just imagine all the women on the planet walking around glowing, simply because they decided to choose fun over anything else! That would be a world worth waking up to!

Goals
are things
men try to
achieve
when they
find women
unsatisfying.

Attributed to
Victor Baranco, Ph.D

Chapter 16

Men Have Given Up and Women Are Resigned

For a lot of men and women, relating has become an unrewarding challenge. It requires too much of our precious time. We've lost interest in continuing down a path we know won't lead to love. People are very disappointed and frustrated with simply getting along and having their needs met. Women feel that men are too much work and they find more fun relating with women friends. When men are with women they wait for the next bomb to drop. They know at any second they could be accused of doing something wrong without ever knowing why. Men are sick and tired of being made wrong by women. Because of this behavior men feel women have become less fun to be around. In turn, men play more sports, work longer hours, put bigger tires on their truck, and add more Ram to their computers. This kind of activity is a safe bet for men to escape any negative accusations.

People can accept only so many failures before relating becomes too much of a hassle. A guy thinks a neat thing to do is buy his woman flowers. On the way home one night he stops at a flower shop, and not knowing what kind she likes, asks the florist for her opinion. She offers some suggestions and he willingly follows her ideas. He takes them home and she says "Oh thank you honey. Those are nice, but next time don't get the baby's breath." He buys her flowers the following week, and he remembers to leave the baby's breath out. She then says, "Wow, I really like these, but I'd prefer pink roses, not red." So after failing to hit a home run several times in a row, he decides the best way to win is to stop bringing her flowers. Sadly this type of scenario happens quite frequently between men and women.

The single population is growing faster than ever before. It's sometimes difficult for newlyweds to be genuinely happy because statistics show that it is just a matter of time before their love may dwindle into the same mire and muck of other failed relationships. A friend of mine is a DJ who understands the man-woman dynamic. She recently told me that she is saddened at weddings she performs for because she knows the couple doesn't have a clue about what to do to have a loving and lasting relationship. She said the greatest wedding gift they could ever receive is a copy of this book!

What most of us don't realize is that the failures and challenges we experience are really wake-up calls for what we need to learn next. The challenges are what make life worth living. If we knew everything we needed to know already, why would we be here? We need to shift our thinking and begin to look at our problems in a new light. Our problems can continue to be problems, or they can be an opportunity to learn. Think about it. If you've had a bad experience, you know you're not going to do that again. You move forward, you've grown and hopefully you're a better person. Too many time, however, we hold these challenges as something bad. We think there must be something wrong with us, or we should have known better when these challenges arise. Each challenge is a gift that puts us more in touch with who we really are and expand our ability to love.

There are many things that are misunderstood in the world. One of the saddest is how completely misunderstood men are by women. It amazes me to see women treat men the way they do. They treat men like total dummies because they really think men are rather ignorant about them. No one really took the time to teach them. Women make men wrong for so many things that are not their fault. Many men are frightened to go near women and have become timid and shy around them. They know women don't understand them. Men wonder why women have never realized how much they want to be her hero.

When a man marries he makes a promise to himself to make his woman happy forever. He often looks at her face to see if she is happy. When a woman is losing and disapproving of her life, he feels like he's failing. He has no way to win and no chance to be her hero. He wants to check out and check out in a hurry. It hurts too much to feel the pain his woman feels. Feeling pain is not one of a man's favorite things - especially emotional pain. They were taught at a young age to stay away from pain. So they will leave in response to a woman not enjoying her life or him. Women need to know that men will stick around when it's fun.

There are many women who are in unhappy relationships or are single by default. Single by default is no fun. It means you are not choosing to be single and don't know what to do to find a mate or keep one. Being single because you want to be is a good thing. The truth is there aren't many women who are single by choice.

Diana was a friend of mine who was single by choice. She loved to go on dinner dates with one man. She had a child with another man. She had another man who took care of her financially and another was a friend she played tennis with. Diana was happy and content with no complaints. This is what she wanted. Women can have all kinds of relationships with men, especially when they lets each one be a hero.

Understanding a woman is a man's biggest challenge. They try over and over to get inside her world, and fail in so many ways that it has become easier to simply tune out. When you ask a man why he got divorced, most of the time the answer is, "I don't know." They never knew what they did or didn't do to have it fall apart. Ultimately what a man can offer a woman is to have her feel fully listened to. Not necessarily to understand her, just to have her feel acknowledged and appreciated.

Women need to be straight and more to the point in their communications with men. This would make them much easier to understand. It is important to speak in a low and slow manner with men. There have been test studies done with men where instructions were delivered by a woman. The higher the pitch of her voice, the less effective men were at following the instructions. Women don't understand how much more effective they could be by talking low and slow with men. And while we are on the subject of slow and low, men don't understand how effective slow and light can be when it comes to having sex with women.

If a woman remembers that men just want to be heroes, she would be smart to speak with them in a direct way about what she wants. It confuses men when women communicate something they want and change how they say it midstream. Slow and low, repeating it three times in the same way, works really well for a man. Slow and low, repeating it three times in the same way, works really well for a man. Slow and low, repeating it three times in the same way, works really well for a man. If you want a man to succeed with your request it's as simple as asking him to pick up the groceries for dinner on the way home from work, followed by leaving him a note in the car with a list of what you need, and then to finally insure his success, and yours, leave him a phone message as well. Oh, and don't forget a big 'thank you' when he comes home with the goodies.

Men and women live in different worlds. Everything about how they operate is different. This is a good thing but it can cause major problems if they don't understand who they are dealing with. Men need to know it's OK that they can't figure out women. It's actually better.

The best that it can get for a man is when he finally accepts he will never figure women out. It's a real challenge for men not being able to get inside a woman's world, however, it is not this way by accident. Actually, understanding women is the booby prize, because if men had it all figured out, there would be no man-woman game to play. In order for a man to win with a woman, he has pay total attention to her. It's the only way he's ever going to begin to know what a woman wants. Total attention from a man is top on a woman's list.

It is strange for a man to hear that it's better not to understand women, because it takes away his illusion of being in control. The truth is he has no control about what goes on in a woman's world. So in order to have a better chance of hitting a home run with her, his best bet is to pay attention to her. Otherwise the man ends up in his head thinking he should know what is going on. Women find this kind of man rather boring and a lot of work and know they are not going to be men who listen to them. They would rather tell a woman what to do than to listen to what she really wants. Once a man realizes there's nothing to figure out, other than to pay attention, they will be greatly relieved. Given a man's goal to succeed they will find a way to win with this new piece of information. ♂♀

A big predicament that we have in the world of man-woman, is that many women have turned into men. Many women have become the producers of everything they want, and are now doing everything for themselves. This is all fine and dandy but when women do a man's job it creates a dynamic that eliminates all the wonderful qualities of a balanced relationship. A balanced relationship is where women are being feminine and men are being manly.

Nothing is worse for a man than to have his woman not desire anything from him. When a man has nothing to do, he becomes stripped of the very essence of what a man is. Men love cycles, anything that has a beginning, middle and an end to it. They love getting to the end of something because they have completed it and that in itself is a win. It is the best when a woman is happy as a result of his production. Men would love to go to their graves a smouldering hulk, all used up. When Suzie knew her man was coming home from an exhausting day at work, she would always look for ways to energize him. He would come in the door and she would say, "Oh honey, I am so happy to see you. Would you please open these jars for me? I can't seem to get them open." He would crank the lids off and feel like a hero. The evening would take off on a different course because she gave him an opportunity to win.

Do you ever wonder why so many men die shortly after they retire? They die because no one has any more use for their production. They feel useless and give up hope because there appears to be no opportunity for them to win anymore.

Women are the most beautiful when they let themselves receive. When women are running around, and intensely working at whatever they are doing, they are not tuned into their feminine power. They are not as beautiful as when they are in the receiving mode. When a man pays quality attention to his woman she responds attractively and her light shines. There is no room for this light to shine when she is deeply involved in a project. She will fail to notice the other half of the population that is willing to lend a hand. If women would look up and see all the capable men out there, they would see the possibility available for them to become women again. They would learn to pleasurably consume a man's production. As long as women continue to do it all themselves, they will continue to blow their chances for any romance.

Women have become more male than female leaving men wondering where all the soft and feminine women have gone. Men would love to see women become more feminine again, because feminine women inspire a man's production. When women learn to use their femininity in a powerful way they will have the answer to the question of how to keep men inspired to produce for them. Sure women can do it themselves. They've proved that by now. When they are doing it all themselves, however, it leaves men with nothing to do. There's no game, no challenge and no way to win. A truly feminine woman is a woman who allows herself to receive. She is the kind of woman who inspires a man to move mountains.

Men want to understand the whole thing; women want to maintain the feminine mystery.

Attributed to
Victor Baranco, Ph.D

Chapter 17

Men and Women are the Same in Different Ways

In the mid eighties I came across a group of people who were having more fun playing with the differences between men and women than I had ever seen. Up until this point, my work had been directed toward the potential of human beings as a species, as opposed to the potential of the genders. This group had discovered a way of relating with the opposite sex that produced more aliveness and self-expression than I had ever experienced. They celebrated and honored our differences instead of being confused and intimidated by them.

I discovered for myself that we are all spiritual beings who simply want to experience love. I also realized, if we wake up every morning and are still in the dark about how to deal with the opposite sex, our difficulty in finding the love we are looking for will be an endless journey.

It's important to understand that men and women live in two different worlds. Our differences are a matter of biology and behavior and do not make one sex superior to the other. One of our main differences in viewing the world is that men are logical and linear, and women are random. The random universe of a woman is bigger than the linear universe of a man. A man has to narrow his focus like a laser beam in order to be productive. A woman's nature is to be random and mercurial, which keeps her moving in many different directions simultaneously. Her random world includes logic. His logical world excludes randomness. This has huge ramifications in attempting to bring our two different worlds together. Men tend to contemplate ideas by themselves and come up with clear and direct answers. Men use very few words. On the other hand, women tend to verbalize everything that is going on in their brain moment to moment. They love to discuss things for hours on end. This is a form of intimacy for a woman. This is a form of insanity for a man.

A man's emotional range is from ho to hum. A woman's is like the ocean with lots of highs and lows. A man prefers and tends to hold a steady state in his emotional range. Men would rather spend as little time as possible in emotional conversations. It is too uncomfortable for them, especially when the conversations are long and drawn out.

Women, on the other hand, like to feel their emotional ups and downs. This is how women know they are alive. If they find life too boring and even keeled they will stir things up just to feel movement again. As a rule, women's lives are generally more emotionally intense than men's.

The Boy Scout Motto is, "I Promise to DO my Best for God and Country." The Girl Scout Motto is, "I Promise to TRY to do my Best." A huge revelation can be made here when you see the impact of this one little word 'try'. There is no TRYing in a man's world. He will DO it, no matter what. Women will TRY, because they don't want to be counted on to keep their word. Women know that men wrote the rules we currently live by. They also know these rules do not take into consideration the random, feeling and emotional nature of a woman. If a woman decides there is a better alternative when she's in the middle of something, she wants to be able to change her mind without being made wrong. So women will TRY, but please, don't count on them.

The mercurial world of a woman includes more cycles than most men care to pay attention to. To relate with a woman, a man has to ignore a lot of her world. He would be overwhelmed if he had to feel everything she feels. However, excluding her world means missing out on many extraordinary experiences that would otherwise be available to him.

The simplicity of a man excludes the complexity of a woman. Look at the names there are for women; magical, bewitching, bedazzling, beguiling, mysterious and enchanting. These are names that conjure up images of something wonderful, but not necessarily understandable. Women are enigmas. They are mysterious without a doubt. It is no wonder men have a difficult time trying to figure them out.

There are different names for men. They are simple, strong, steadfast and dependable. The names for men are more grounded and give the feeling of certainty. The perfectly grounded man balances the perfectly mysterious woman.

A man's existence shows up as simple to a woman. Whether he's getting his meals, working on projects, or finding things in the same place; it's a life a man prefers to have in black or white. This is a huge contrast to the full spectrum of color a woman prefers to live in. A man's day is usually the same in the evening as it was in the morning. Their whole day is pretty much the same. They try to make each day better and better, to insure that in a year or so they will have a pretty good life, and hope it will stay that way. Steady as she goes is what a man loves. A man's world may be more mundane, but they like it that way.

This steady state is what supports a man in tough times. When a woman wants to pull her hair out, this is where a man can help. He can stabilize the situation. When there are disasters, like a hurricane, men always come through. They complete whatever cycle they are on. They disown the rest of the universe and focus on what's in front of them to get the job done.

Women like their lives to be a never-ending date. They love dates because, hopefully, the attention is all on them. Have you ever heard the expression, 'women go first in pleasure' and 'men go first in danger'? Women love to be ushered ahead of a man, when escorted to their seats in a restaurant. They love to show off how they look with their special guy close behind. On the other hand, if women are on a crowded street, they love their man to go first to protect them from the crowd. This is chivalry in the 21st century. Chivalry is not dead.

Women love to be at the receiving end of the pleasurable things men do for them. When you hear a woman recall a date with a man, she always speaks from the place of being the receiver. She says, "He brought me flowers, and then he opened all my doors, and then he took me to this awesome restaurant, and then he bought me this lovely gift", etc. Her face lights up recalling the date, because she is recalling being totally taken care of. This continues the excitement in her mind of what's to come in future. His gifts of attention on her are key to her wanting him more.

When you hear a man recall a date, he says, "Well I got her some flowers, and I took her to Spazio's, and I bought the best bottle of wine, and I took her dancing." He did, he did, he did, for her. Men like to be the producers. They like to cause the action. That's what they are best at. Women like to be at the effect of a man's pleasurable actions. That's when a woman feels most like a woman.

Chivalry is all about women wanting to be at effect, because there is more drama, energy and excitement this way. If women are at cause for making things happen, there is no way for them to receive. If you want a woman to be happy, put her at effect.

Men are mystified why women want all the attention that they want. Women want attention in the worst way. Unfortunately, that's how they sometimes get it, in the worst way. Men don't understand why women want so much attention. Too much attention on a man makes him very feel uncomfortable. Men like attention on their production, not their person. They love to hear a woman praise what they've accomplished, but can only take a little attention on how they look.

If a man goes to a spa, he can only have attention on his body for one or two treatments. Then he feels he has to go out and produce something. He is not comfortable being on the receiving end for an extended period of time. He is mostly empowered when he is at cause.

Attention is very grounding to a woman. Many times, women are not in their bodies. They are moving so fast with all the things they have their attention on they become very ungrounded. Any kind of attention she receives from a man is grounding to her. A simple hug can do wonders. A woman is calmer when she's grounded and, therefore, much nicer to be around. A woman's body and everything about her is like a man's car is to him. This is the hand she's been dealt to play on the game board of life. Anything that a man notices with appreciation validates the very essence of who she is. Women can have a man acknowledge everything he likes about her from head to toe, and she will still have room for more. Women can never get too many sincere compliments.

♂♀

When a couple has had an argument, and the man is feeling hurt, a woman needs to remember that he doesn't bounce back as quickly as she does. Men need more time to recover when their feelings are hurt. When women look at the expression on their man's face, they will see the effect of their handiwork. If he has not recovered from the argument, he will not be willing to engage.

This can drive a woman crazy. A woman can beat a man up for something he probably didn't know he did, and then look at his face and feel guilty about what she has done. A woman needs to realize the fastest way to have her man come back from an argument, is for her to put her attention on enjoying herself. She has to move away from what she has done and move towards having her own good time. This will make the man respond to her more quickly than anything else. She has to give up trying to change how he's feeling. That never works. That is more torture for him. She also has to give up any guilt she has for causing the incident in the first place. She needs to realize that a man knows when a woman is genuinely happy. Only then, will it feel safe for him to come out and play again.

Ted and Alice lived in Seattle with their roommate Nicole. One day Ted and Alice had a big argument where some painful things were said. Ted's feelings were hurt in a big way. Alice took off, went to a coffee shop and ran into Nicole. Alice never mentioned the fight to Nicole. When Nicole came home later, she saw Ted looking very down and out. She asked him what was wrong. He said, "Alice and I had a terrible fight and she stormed off a few hours ago." Nicole said, "Well I just ran into her at Starbucks and she looked happy to me."

The point I am making here is that men take longer to recover from arguments than women do. They don't bounce back until it feels safe for them. Women don't have to wait for a man to feel better. They can simply flip their switch and have their attention on something much more fun. Men need it to feel safe before they come out and play again. Safe, for a man, would be for a woman to show up happy again. A man will always follow a woman's lead, especially, when it leads to more fun.

♂♀

There is nothing a man can do that a woman couldn't do as well. However, there are many physical jobs that women aren't interested in taking on. Too few women have realized how lucky they are that men utilize their strengths to literally move the mountains they do. Women are demonstrating they can do jobs as well as men, and sometimes, even better, by showing up as doctors, lawyers, senators and pilots.

Self-realized women know they are superior to men. A woman's ability to intuit the world around her gives her an edge that men, in their logical world, will never have. This edge allows them to see the bigger picture, which enables them to be better planners. They use their vision to see what's best for all concerned and anticipate any problems that may surface.

Women know they are smarter than men, but not necessarily better. This, by the way, is the reason women find it difficult to surrender to men. How could women surrender to someone they think is inferior? Women finally surrender to men because they know they will gain something by doing so. Women want men to assist them in achieving their goals.

If you leave a bunch of men alone on a deserted island, they'd handle their basics, but wouldn't do much more. However, add a woman to the mix, and in a very short period of time, the island would be converted to a resort complete with running water, grass shack, sushi bar and pina coladas. Women like to live more comfortably than men. It's always been the woman's desire that has inspired men to produce the kinds of things we have in our world today.

Women are the ones who are going to move the world toward more love and compassion. The only way women will be able to bridge the gap between the sexes, is to use their feminine power in a more loving way. Women need to direct their love and compassion toward men to enable them to understand women better. This is the only way we will ever be the perfect partners we were meant to be for each other. We have to celebrate how different we are, and we have to recognize that ultimately we all want the same thing - to be happy and to be loved.

If you
can't have
romance
here and now,
you can't
get it there
and then.

Attributed to
Victor Baranco, Ph.D

Chapter **18**

Got Intimacy?

Everyone seems to want more intimacy and at the same time everyone is afraid of it. To be intimate means to be willing to reveal sides of yourself that could be judged or evaluated. It can be a scary thing. What if someone judged you when you were vulnerable? What if you thought you could trust a person but were betrayed? Could you ever share yourself again?

One of the most precious things about relating with someone in an intimate way is the sweetness that occurs in the moment of sharing. It's the closeness and the connection that is so important to us. We thrive on it. Intimacy makes us feel connected to our partner in a much deeper way. To be intimate with someone means to be with a person who knows you and loves you just the way you are.

To have intimacy you need to be open and present in a nonthreatening way. There must be no secrets. It has to feel safe. There must be total trust between two people. If you don't know where the other person stands, intimacy will go out the window. When women don't have intimacy in a relationship they will start to complain and get rather cantankerous.

135

The opportunities for intimacy are everywhere, especially when you're happy with yourself. Most people think of sex when they think of being intimate, because they think sex is the only way to be intimate. When you break down the word intimacy it becomes IN TO ME SEE. It means to look deeper into yourself and you will have more intimacy. It can become the simple act of expressing yourself in the moment. The bedroom is not the only place where two people can genuinely share themselves. While everyone is looking for moments of deep connection the first thing we need to do, is realize that intimacy can happen anywhere with anyone at anytime.

Intimacy happens in the moment of sharing your vulnerability. You can sit at the kitchen table and gaze sweetly into the eyes of a friend. It's happens when you express your desire and willingness to connect. You can communicate that you are open and love being with them through your eyes alone. They approve of you and you approve of them. This can become a soul connection if you're willing to let it in. That's intimacy. It's not difficult but requires being very present and willing to be vulnerable.

If you want more intimacy in your life, begin by accepting yourself. It will allow you to put attention on someone outside of yourself. It's difficult to be intimate with someone, if you're judging and evaluating everything about yourself. We have to remember each of us is perfect no matter what past actions we've taken. If we're doing the best we know how at any given moment, how can we ever be wrong?

People get a lot of mileage out of thinking negatively about themselves and miss the sweet things in life. They end up wasting precious time thinking they are somehow wrong. Intimacy will never work with this kind of thinking. Give up judging and you'll find many more opportunities for intimacy. If you don't have a connection with yourself, it's impossible to have one with someone else. Remember, everyone is being the most loving they know how to be with their current level of awareness. Fortunately, there's always more love to experience.

If we don't give ourselves permission to be who we are, there will be no opening for anyone to be intimate with us. There will be no one to be with, period, if you're someone who judges themselves. Many people are too hard on themselves. They beat themselves up for everything and think they should be some other way. They never give themselves a break. They will stay stuck as long as they put themselves down.

If you want to change this, notice when you put yourself down. Acknowledge that you did this, and don't resist it. Remember, what you resist persists. The next step is to find something you like about what just happened. Be grateful for the fact that you are becoming more of an observer in life, and less of a victim of your own thinking. That's the intimacy you can have with yourself. This exercise will prepare you to be intimate with another.

One of the things I hear from women, is how much they love it when their man simply enjoys spending time with them. This means he's happy to put attention on things that matter to her. A woman loves it when a man is willing to go with her flow. It gives an ordinary moment more intimacy when a man is willing to follow her activity and enjoy whatever she's doing. Sometimes this is a challenge for men, because they usually think they are responsible for the woman's happiness. If there is nothing a woman wants other than for him to be with her, he can easily feel useless. Since men are use to producing, they may feel uncomfortable, when the only use for them is to simply be present.

Share yourself fully, with no attachment, if there is something you want to share with your partner. Do it openly and completely with no expectations. Many times men and women make the mistake of expecting their partner to reciprocate in some way. It will feel like manipulation if you have an agenda. When your partner sees you expressing yourself because you truly want to, it may become a catalyst for your partner to do the same. If you let your partner know how much you appreciate their attentiveness, they will feel comfortable being with you. Getting the crowbar out and expecting your partner to share, never forwards the goal of having more intimacy.

Nothing is more attractive than people who are willing to be real. We have to dare to share our true nature with our friends and our partner. Why? Because when people are willing to tell it like it is, from their heart, it inspires others to be more real themselves. Real is where it's at. When you are honest and genuine, you honor yourself. Speaking your truth and expressing yourself in a loving way shows vulnerability. It takes courage and is always attractive.

Women need to remember it's not easy for men to be intimate and vulnerable. Women are unaware of the box they've kept men in. Men have been judged heavily by society and are considered weak if they express their love in tender and affectionate ways. How does a woman make it easy for a man to let down his guard? By being vulnerable herself.

A man's role has been that of the provider. They shoulder the responsibility of having to know all the right answers. Women now need to take responsibility for showing men how to be intimate. They need to nurture the sensitive, caring side of men and make it safe for them to reveal themselves. It's a function of safety for a man. If he knows he's not going to be judged, he will feel freer to open up and be vulnerable. Women need to stop trying to change men and learn to work with their vulnerabilities.

Opportunities for intimacy can exist outside our personal relationships. Women, for example, love to be intimate with everything that surrounds them. This is why women love puppies, fragrant flowers, spectacular sunsets and romantic songs. Women feel a unique connection with their surroundings, which allows them to have what feels like a spiritual experience. When women see and appreciate the everyday gifts life has to offer, life becomes more intimate. Filling their lives with pleasurable experiences make women happier and healthier and have them feel more intimately connected to everything.

If we can learn to live each moment as if it were our last, we would relate with everyone we meet in a completely different way. We would connect in a more compassionate and reverent way with whomever we meet. Every human being is valuable and unique and worthy of unconditional love and respect.

Adopting this kind of attitude about the people we meet would open more doors and provide a life worth waking up to every morning. Everyone deserves a smile and the time of day. One never knows if the next person they meet will be a connection that lasts a lifetime, a season, or a brief but special moment. Our prayers are always being answered. What you've been praying for may be the next person you meet.

We are all writing our own script called 'being human'. Look at it this way. We are in the school of life every day we're alive. It is here we learn our lessons on how to be happy. The only person who is always going to be with you is YOU. Be happy with yourself everyday you're alive. Find reasons to engage with the world around you, even if it's as simple as waving to someone. A simple hello or smile has the power to totally change someone's day. You can end each day knowing you got the most out of your Human Being 101 class. If you're conscious and awake you'll get an "A" every day. It's your life – you are writing the script everyday. The question is, "How much fun and intimacy are you having with the script you've written?" If you're not having fun, write a new scene.

What's the worst thing that could happen if you were to be real with someone? Perhaps they would judge you in a negative way. Perhaps they would choose not to relate with you. It might be their loss but it won't be yours. No one can ever negate the heart and soul of who you are. You are everlasting love. When you live from this knowing, it doesn't matter if anyone judges you. What matters is that you love yourself.

When you know you are love, you become one with the world around you. You experience the world as part of you, and relate with it in a more intimate way. You realize that whatever you do to another, you are actually doing to yourself. When you have fun with someone else, it's the same as having fun with yourself. Go out and have fun and don't be afraid to be vulnerable and real. Life is not about what you say or what you do, as much as who you are being in the moment. When you are completely real, you will become intimately connected with everything around you. It's that simple. It's time to get real!

Efficiency
is not
romantic.
Romance
is
efficient.

Attributed to
Victor Baranco, Ph.D

Chapter 19

The Difference Between Sex and Sensuality

A common misnomer among many people is that sensuality and sexuality are one in the same. The dictionary defines sensuality as 'relating to or consisting in the gratification of the senses, or the indulgence of appetite'. Even though men may think they are satisfying a woman's sensual needs by being sexual with her, most women today do not feel satisfied in their sensual lives with men.

Women want to experience being loved by a sensitive man - a sensitive, Renaissance man. They have to keep in mind that men are anxious to satisfy women any way they can, but have been inadequate in understanding how sensual woman are. If women want to have satisfying sensual lives with men, they will need to educate them about the importance of paying attention to the senses.

A woman's focus is mostly on her sensual world. The perfumes she smells, fabrics she feels, songs that move her, sunsets that inspire her and chocolates that tantalize her taste buds, are the kinds of things that will arouse her senses. No one does sensuality better than a woman. She appreciates anything and everything that feeds her senses. Men need to be aware of how important a woman's sensual life is to her. Realizing that men and women operate on very different channels is the first step to having a sex life full of passion, love and aliveness and love.

Women's lives are oriented around the present time enjoyment of all their senses. When their senses are pleasurably stimulated, they experience being more sensual. It's easier for women to be more sexual when they are in touch with their senses. Women are always interested in how it feels to their senses; how it feels NOW. They instinctively feel everything that goes on in each moment.

A woman can feel when a man really wants to be with her, or whether he simply wants to get her into bed. One of the frequent complaints you hear from women about their sex life is how focused men are on getting off. Men 'go for the goal' to move their energy. They want to release this energy, so they can return to work and focus on their life again. Achieving 'the goal' helps them clear their mind.

Being with a woman usually includes a lot more cycles, many of which turn into a whole string of complexities. Remember all those buttons, levers and dials? Well men just want to reset the counter. They are wired to complete things. Once they start, they want to finish.

Women, on the other hand, focus on their senses each moment. She notices right away when his attention is somewhere else. Whether they are talking, dancing, kissing, or in the throws of wild passionate love making, if he is not present to her, she is thinking, "Hellooo, is anybody home?" You can't fool a woman in this area. She knows without a doubt, when a man is not there.

When a man is fully present it always feels good to the woman, no matter how skilled he may be in the art of pleasuring her. She will automatically want the next caress or kiss. It feels safe to her because she can trust him. She knows she won't be hurt because he is fully present with her.

If a man is interested in what he might get in the future, instead of enjoying her in the moment, he will have a frustrated woman on his hands. Going through the motions is not satisfying for either sex, although men are less likely to complain. Many female problems are the result of the woman having sex that doesn't feel good to her. She doesn't know how to tell a man to slow down, get present, or stop. Sometimes it doesn't feel good to her but not knowing how to say what she wants, continues to have sex. Eventually, if a woman doesn't speak up her body will communicate for her. This is a common cause of urinary tract infections and yeast infections.

Men and women settle for a quality of sex that is light years from what it could be. A simple shift in the understanding of who you are sharing your bed with will make all the difference. When men realize a woman's mode of operating is very different than theirs, they will begin to gain some clarity on how to truly pleasure her. We've been trying to have Romeo and Juliett get it together, and haven't realized that Juliett only lives in present time, while ol' Romeo is simply working on how to climb up the rope to get her into bed. Thank heavens Romeo and every other man have the ability to follow instructions. Some simple verbal guidance from the Juliets of the world will do wonders to move everyone in the direction of more pleasure.

Men bring romance looking for sex. Women bring sex looking for romance. A really good day for a man would include some sort of sexual gratification. Women don't understand why men want it so much. They don't see that it's just the nature of the beast. Sometimes it appears as though men only want sex and are not interested in romance. The truth is, men would love to be romantic, but need an attractive invitation. A woman should know that if a man perceives the promise of sex some time in the future, he will be more than willing to shower a woman with romance.

Men have to be vulnerable to show their romantic side. It hasn't been safe for them to do this. They have been devastated one way or another by women. It's been much easier for men to non-confront romance and just go for 'the goal'. They don't realize, however, how much this costs them.

Women want to be genuinely ravished and romanced by men. They would love a man to be romantic if he thoroughly enjoyed displaying this kind of affection. When a woman knows a man truly enjoys giving to her in romantic ways, she finds it much easier to let his affections in. Romance is one of a woman's favorite kinds of foreplay. When women receive the romance they want, it's almost a guarantee the man will get what he wants.

Women need to know that men are very capable of being romantic. However, in order for men to develop their 'romance' muscle, they need to be inspired. Romance is a special space a man holds. It's the space of, 'This is my queen, my goddess. I put her on a pedestal'.

Men are afraid to let out a little romance because it may all come pouring out. They're like a wooden barrel with rings around it. If you loosen one of the rings, everything may spill out. It can be a frightening tunnel for a man to venture down, especially if he doesn't know his woman's particular likes and dislikes. Any time he chances being romantic with her, he risks the possibility of failing - of doing it wrong. He might bring her flowers she doesn't like, or light aroma therapy candles at dinner, not knowing she is allergic to fragrances.

If women knew men just want to win, they would be more sensitive and appreciative of the things men do for them. When men experience winning enough times with the little things they do, they will be likely to venture into more risky areas. Just remember, when it's safe for men with no fear of reprisal, they will be willing to play. They will play like Olympians if they know they won't be made wrong for their efforts.

The man woman dynamic is really designed to have both sides win and get everything they want. However, a woman must be heard first. When a woman knows a man has heard her, she will open, soften and be much more willing to meet her man's needs. It's ladies first. Women's needs have been ignored for too long. It would be good for men to know, if they give women what they want in the beginning, women will give back to them 100%. It's the easiest way for men to get what they want, too. Simply listen fully to what a woman is saying and quickly respond to her communication. This is the kind of attention women want. It will make it easier for her to talk with him in the future.

It becomes very tiring for a woman, if a man's ego gets in the way of what she wants. If this happens too often, she will eventually give up asking for anything. They will both lose at this point. A man needs to be grateful when his woman tells him how he can win with her. We all know, when men discover what women want, there will be a much bigger chance of everyone being happy.

♂♀

Men and women are born for love. Kisses are preludes to love, true love. It is a starting point of sexual love. For this reason, the manner in which a kiss is performed is vitally important. Kisses really count when love is present. Love is an essential ingredient of a satisfying kiss. Kisses can be blissful, or empty and meaningless. One thing for sure, they are an absolute essential to a happy relationship. No kissing, no happy!

People kiss to satisfy a hunger that is as natural as breathing. The ongoing hunger we have to connect sexually is what drives us to each other. The instant a pair of lips touch, many things are communicated. A man and woman know in a moment whether the person they are kissing is someone they are interested in as a romantic partner. A kiss reveals who a person is, whether they are present, and if there's any magical attraction.

Remember what it was like when you were anticipating the first kiss from your lover? Next time your partner reaches to kiss you, gently hold them back with your hand while looking into their eyes. Don't say a thing. Rather, look deep into their eyes as they gaze back at you. Move closer to them and with one finger, trace the shape of their face, around their eyes, and their nose, and then slowly over their lips and down their chin. Bring their face close to yours. Slowly bring your lips to theirs, softly kissing only the upper lip, then the lower. Then bring your arms around them, slowly let the kiss grow, lips parting, until both of you are washed away with passion. When the kiss stops, remain in the embrace. Look deeply into their eyes again before ending the embrace. It doesn't matter if you have been married twenty days or twenty years. When you take the time to really kiss your partner, the response is always a good one.

Kisses can never be defined, but kisses that aren't enjoyed in the moment are a huge waste of time. If you are not enjoying kissing, you won't be enjoying the next part of the sexual adventure either. Too many men pass over the importance kissing is to a woman. They put little attention there, thinking what she wants is the big "O". Women will only get to the big "O" when every act, including the first kiss, is one that turns them on.

One thing women freely share with each other is how great, or not so great, a man is at kissing. A good kisser is a vital requirement for a woman. Women will actually bring a potential relationship to a complete and total halt after experiencing the initial kiss if it's totally unsatisfactory. It is sad but it is true. Women think if a man is an unskilled kisser, coupled with no connection or spark - to go any further would be pointless. A secret not many women know is that all men are trainable, even in the kissing department.

A woman could kiss a great kisser all night long. She wouldn't need, or want, to come up for air. Kisses are the language of love. It is very sensual and romantic for a woman to be exquisitely lost in a kiss with her man. No two people are alike and no two kisses are alike. People make kisses. To be willing to be present enough to spend an evening experiencing the many delicious kinds of kisses, is the difference between sensuality and sexuality.

My life
is great
and
it's all
your fault.

Attributed to
Victor Baranco, Ph.D

Chapter **20**

Tame the Blame Game

Here we are in the 21st century thinking we are more evolved than we've ever been, yet it is amazing how often men and women continue making each other wrong. Instead of enjoying loving and nurturing connections, we have been faced with a series of frustrating, confusing and bewildering associations. There is a major misunderstanding between men and women, which needs to be revealed and made clear to avoid further stress and pain.

The design of man-woman is actually perfect. It's yin and yang. We fit together perfectly but rarely experience this to be true. We never took Relationships 101. It was never offered. Mom and dad just assumed we should know what to do to have successful relationships. Unfortunately, our only role models were our parents who learned about relating from their parents. Dad's job was to protect the family and bring home a paycheck and Mom's was to feed and raise the family. The roles of husband and wife were clearly defined.

Mankind has evolved over the years and the rules have changed. The world is no longer run by men alone. Our former role models no longer serve us. In the days when we were growing up with our parents it was a man's world where women were to be seen and not heard. The way our parents related was perfect for their time, but it is no longer useful in this day and age. The time is now for women to speak up and be heard. Women are beginning to achieve success on a whole new level and intend to have an equal voice.

When you observe the way men and women relate today, it becomes easy to understand why so many relationships fail. Many couples don't even get to first base. People are taking seminars and therapy to try to 'fix' whatever problems they think they have. I am not saying that seminars and therapy don't have value. It's just that people aren't broken and don't need fixing. When human beings try to fix themselves they become much less attractive to the opposite sex.

If you're trying to fix yourself it means you think there's something wrong with you. The real truth is, there's nothing 'wrong' with you or anyone else. Thinking you are wrong is one of the most un-empowering thoughts you can have. You are already perfect but haven't learned to accept it. To know you're perfect means you accept yourself just the way you are. When you accept yourself just the way you are it becomes much easier to have more loving viewpoints about your partner.

In order for relationships to thrive and flourish, we need to learn how to love and embrace the differences between the sexes. No doubt you've seen the picture of the panels on the cover of this book. This is a perfect illustration of why men and women have not learned how to achieve the loving connection they want. It points to profound differences that until now have gone unacknowledged.

Women have 30 - 40 buttons, levers and dials, and can't believe that men only have one. The fact that men really are that simple and uncomplicated is mind-boggling to women.

Men are simply trying to understand the world of women through their one button called "Does this feel good or does this feel bad? Are we winning? Or are we losing?" Women are impossible to understand. Men will never be able to figure them out. You may read this and laugh, but it's really the nuts and bolts of why there is such a breakdown in relationships. It's not that men are, in any way, less than women. It's that women are more complex than men realize.

Our differences are not the problem. They are the opening and the opportunity to connect. Men and women are the perfect compliment for each other. If we're relating to each other as if our differences are the problem, we will be in deep trouble. In reality, it's our differences that give the power to the man-woman dynamic.

Women operate with many buttons, levers, and dials and many of them are all working at the same time. They are multi-tasking creatures. They're all over the map and like it that way. Men on the other hand are logical, linear creatures. They like to put one foot in front of the other and get to where they're going. They like to live simply with logic and order. This reminds me of a story about a man I knew who worked as a postman. He would put the paychecks he'd get every two weeks on top of the refrigerator. Life was simple. If he ever needed money he took one of the checks and cashed it. Over the years this stack grew considerably. Then one day he met the love of his life and married her. The checks quickly disappeared. Every day he would come home and notice there was something new like curtains, area rugs, sofas, chairs, bedding. You name it, she bought it. Men are happy to live with the basics, but a woman's needs are much more complex.

The random world of women includes the ability to be logical. The logical world of men, however, cannot include the multi-tasked world of women. Random-ability includes all logicalness. Logicalness excludes random-ability. This means women have the ability to understand men and the 'manese' language. Men do not have the ability to understand women and the 'womanese' language. However, women have a hard time believing men could be so simple. Women think since men are so brilliant at creating and inventing things, they must also be able to understand the female species more than they do. You will find out later that this misconception about men is one of the main reasons for the breakdowns in relationships.

It can be very frustrating to a man to try to figure women out. Both sexes have made each other wrong for so long they don't even know who they are anymore. Yes, women are all over the map. They have fun being this way because it is their nature. Women can't imagine being logical and linear all the time like men. It would be incredibly boring to a her. On the other hand, men cannot imagine living like women do. It would be totally exhausting to them. Men like being grounded and certain of what they're going to do next, while women like to be more spontaneous.

If we're ever going to bridge the gap we will need to find more ways to have fun with how different we are. We have to learn to capitalize on our differences. For instance, women can utilize a lot of the masculine qualities of a man, like his drive to complete projects, his steadfastness and his problem solving. On the other hand, men can benefit from the love and nurturing of a woman. We've put much attention on how we want to change each other and not enough attention on how great it is that men are simple and women are complex. Men are uncomplicated compared to women. They just want approval. They want to win. They are not a big mystery.

We need to celebrate our differences because they are the key to having the kind of relationships we want. Without learning that our differences can give us everything we've been looking for, we are doomed to have failed relationships and a divorce rate that continues to skyrocket. Mankind needs to embrace this simple concept of accepting and honoring just how different we are. We are all pretty exasperated from everything we've tried up to now to bridge the gap between men and women. But if your goal is to have fun in life, the best way is to learn everything you can about our differences. You have the manual to 'more fun' in your hands right now. Keep reading and you will be pleasantly surprised at how simple it is for both sides to win and win big!

Actually, it's so simple we have missed it! Relating has been difficult because we haven't had the tools and understanding that we've so badly needed. We have been looking in all the wrong places. We've been looking outside of ourselves, trying to fix our partners, while the solutions have been right in front of us. This reminds me of my friend Suzie who was always working on Brad to get more organized. The more she worked on trying to change him the worse he got. As soon as she accepted his disorganized ways, they were able to sit down and work out their challenges in a way that allowed him to be himself. We need to give up thinking that anybody needs changing. We would do our relationships a big favor if we would see that people are simply doing the best they know how.

In the greater scheme of things, life is constantly evolving. We are never wrong for whatever choices we make in any particular moment. We're intelligent creatures. We've connected the whole world via the internet and haven't figured out how to artfully master the task of creating successful, loving, joy filled relationships. We are just human beings trying to figure out the best way to live our lives.

The probability of world peace without understanding our differences is very unlikely. How do we ever expect to live in a peaceful world if men and women aren't getting along? The simple but profound distinctions this book reveals will give you the keys to the ultimate connection we all want. World peace begins the minute we decide to embrace our differences and Tame The Blame Game. Just imagine happy and empowered men and women everywhere. This would create a peaceful world without a doubt.

The
best way
to
proceed
is
to play.

Attributed to
Victor Baranco, Ph.D

Chapter 21

Spontaneous Funbustion

I have been accused by many of being 'the most fun person they've met in years'. It comes as no surprise to me because I make it a point to interact with people and life in playful and fun ways. I am always looking for ways to inspire people to have more fun with what's in front of them. I love to observe people and how they react to their life situations. By making fun and playfulness a priority in each moment life ends up coming much more enjoyable.

Spontaneity is the name of the game. It's your ability to be spontaneous with what's in front of you that makes the difference between a happy life, or a life of simply going through the motions. It's about going with the flow in life. Spontaneity will bring lightness, playfulness, and unexpected enjoyment to any circumstance you find yourself in. It will wake up a potentially boring relationship. You must make it a priority to be spontaneous if you want to have any fun in your relationships. When you adopt a lighthearted attitude you will feel more vibrant and youthful. You will be more fun for your partner to enjoy.

Being spontaneous means never getting bored. Most people have no 'spontaneity' muscle, which is why so many people are bored with their lives. Their lives are run on automatic pilot. Boredom comes from their unwillingness to put attention on something outside of themselves. If you take any object and put your attention on it you can observe many things about it. You can do the same with human beings. If you are bored and life feels a little flat, you can turn this around by putting your attention on someone and notice what you like about them. You can do this with anyone at any time. The trouble is we are lazy and haven't exercised this muscle very much. People don't realize, when they are bored, it's usually because all their attention is on themselves.

Since 9/11, human beings have realized the necessity of reevaluating their lives. People are beginning to see that life is too short to miss the joy that is available in each moment. It is time to lighten up and get out of the 'serious' box we've been living in. It doesn't do anyone any good to focus on what's not working in our lives. We need to stop making unfavorable situations worse by feeling bad about them. Some people think if they suffer long enough about something, the problem will go away. Not so. If you suffer for a long time about something, you will actually perpetuate it. There are no victims here. What you resist persists. If you are going to have any fun in life, you need to take responsibility for the fact that you create it. You are literally doing everything to yourself.

Life is 10% what happens to you and 90% how you choose to react to it. Life continues to happen moment by moment. No matter what we may think, we are always making choices about how to experience our lives. The question is, are you choosing a fun, upbeat, and positive life, or a drab, depressed and boring one?

You have a choice, why not choose fun? You can choose to see the positive aspects of anything or the negative ones. People who focus on the good in every situation, are clearly the ones who are having more fun. Is there some other goal in life than to enjoy it? When you're committed to seeing the good in everything, what you end up with is a lot of good in your life. The reverse is also true. How simple is that?

On some level, nothing means anything - except the meaning we give to it. We have to learn to take a step back and become an observer in our lives, to avoid losing sight of the bigger picture of why we're all here.

The purpose of life is to be happy. Life can become pretty routine and dreary when you don't take time to enjoy yourself. Today could be the last day of your life - you never know when our time is up. If you learn to be more spontaneous you will end up with a life rich in precious experiences - a life full of happy moments with no regrets.

Whenever you do something nice for someone, you feel better about yourself and more connected to that person. When was the last time you paid for the toll for the person behind you? Or the last time you left a post-it note with a sweet message on it for a friend? When was the last time you complemented a stranger? Practicing random acts of kindness is loving spontaneity in its purest form. It's a way of loving your self more. When we are loving ourselves, it's natural to want to give some of this love to others.

Live your life like there's no tomorrow - there are no guarantees you'll wake up in the morning. Do you go to sleep at night with a smile on your face and song in your heart? Are you complete with the people you love in your life? Do you tell your partner you love them before you fall off to sleep? Are you present to the fact that every moment of your life is a gift? Are you laughing enough in your life? You should be because THIS IS IT! This is how life has turned out for you at this moment in time. Are you satisfied with it or do you want more? Remember life is not a dress rehearsal.

Do you give yourself permission to turn off your phones and go golfing, or go to the beach, or get a massage? Do you actually go on the romantic weekend you've promised yourself for years? Do you send your mother flowers for no reason? Do you get up early to watch the sunrise or make time to see the sunset? If not now, when?

Human beings operate as if they have all the time in the world to express how much their friends and family mean to them. A simple spontaneous call to someone you love, telling them how much they mean to you, will alter their life and warm your heart. It will create the connection that you and every other human being is always seeking. It's the connection we have with other human beings that matters most.

Why are you waiting to make that call? Tomorrow may never come for that person. Stop ignoring the things you know would impact everybody's life in a more positive way. When you're willing to live your life like there's no tomorrow, you will be living a life you've always dreamed of. The world will benefit greatly when everyone takes responsibility for the fact that today is the only day there is. THIS IS IT! THERE'S ONLY NOW! ♂♀

Everyone on the planet appreciates humor. We need to have more humor in our relationships. It is so important to people, they are willing to pay for it at comedy clubs. Humor is a universal language that occurs in the moment when we least expect it. Humor in our lives is nourishing to our body, mind and spirit. It makes the difference between a boring relationship and a fun one. To have more laughter and joy in your life learn to make fun and light out of life. Let go of any expectations and go with the flow.

Everyone loves to be around people with a great sense of humor. They make us forget all our troubles and worries and put us in the present moment. Laughter is a very important quality for successful relating and will help relationships stay vibrant and alive. Every relationship needs to have a frequent dose of humor in order to survive the normal course of ups and downs. If you don't have humor in your life, what do you have? All great relationships have a foundation of humor.

Humor is the ability to focus on the subtle, or not so subtle, events in our lives through glasses with less serious lenses. You will find many reasons to laugh at yourself if you get into present time and take a look around at what you've created in your life. It can be as significant or insignificant as you choose. Remember nothing means anything except what you decide it means. If you can laugh at yourself you will be free to be yourself. If you can't laugh at yourself, who and what are you trying to be? Give it up and get real! Life is too short to carry on a facade. Who are you trying to impress? The only one you need to impress is yourself. Impress yourself with total love and acceptance and you will be able to enjoy everything around you. My father use to always quote the famous line, "Laugh and the world laughs with you. Cry and you cry alone".

What would happen if you didn't care what other people thought about you? You would be free to be yourself. This might look foolish at times, but you would have a good time. Like the guy at the party with the lamp shade on his head - he may look foolish, but he's definitely having fun.

To get what
you want
you're going
to have to do
whatever
it takes,
even if it
means
being
happy.

Attributed to
Victor Baranco, Ph.D

Chapter 22

Women Want Sex, Food and Baubles

The complex world of a woman includes many conversations around these three categories. There is a hierarchy to the order of what it takes to make a woman happy. In order for men to succeed in making women happy, they will need to learn these simple truths.

It is easy for a man to please a woman when he is privy to which category needs attention. Everything a woman wants is covered in these three categories; connection (sex), food and baubles. If a man's goal is to make a woman happy, it's a waste of time to put attention on the wrong category.

There are certain things women must have in their relationships with men that no amount of money can buy. Feeling a connection with a man is on the top of a woman's list. This feeling of connection is what makes every aspect of the relationship work. Another name for the 'Connection' category is the 'Sex' category. I call it connection rather than sex, because women aren't interested in having sex without the connection. Sex is a form of communication that is highly overrated. It's more important to a woman to feel connected to her man than to have sex night after night with no connection. Men need to know there's more to being connected with a woman than sex. As a matter of fact, the act of intercourse is at the bottom of her most important category - the 'Connection' or 'Sex' category.

Communication is what makes a woman feel connected to her partner. Open and honest communication. Sex is a form of communication. Women have a difficult time having sex when communication is missing. How can you communicate inside the bedroom when it's not happening outside the bedroom?

Everything in a man-woman relationship is about how it 'feels' to a woman. When a woman feels a man respects her, by listening to her, she feels safe enough to entertain being intimate with him. Women dislike being touched when it's apparent the man isn't listening to her. A woman knows a man is insensitive when he is unaware and uninterested in how she feels. If he is not sensitive to her needs, she will regret having sex with him. She will just be going through the motions, which will be very unsatisfying. On a subconscious level she will disapprove of him. The truth is she's disapproving of herself for not following her own inner guidance in the first place. Her guidance is saying, 'See me, hear me, feel me - then touch me'.

Women want friendship first, then a man's physical attention. It makes them feel safe knowing that he would also be happy to be friends first. If their relating turned out to be nothing more than a friendship, and a woman knew from the beginning he'd be okay with that, it would make her more comfortable to be around him. A woman has to honor what she feels because if there is no connection, there's no possibility for a sexual relationship. Women tend to feel bad when the connection is not there especially when they know the man would like to be intimate with them. However, no one can make themselves feel something that's not there.

Many times women would like to have man friends, but are let down, because most men are unwilling to be friends, if there's no sex involved. It's rare to find a man who is willing to be friends with a woman he's attracted to, when sex is not on the menu. Some men say they would like more women friends. If that is truly what they want, they need to put all their sexual comments and innuendos aside. It's a drain for woman to have to be on guard against those kinds of comments. If a man really honors the woman's choice, however, she will respect him more, and in turn will keep her eyes open for a potential mate for him.

When a woman feels connected to her partner, she will more likely be open to intimacy. Women have to feel connected to their man. It's too frightening otherwise. It reminds them of all the times when they were younger, and had sex they didn't enjoy. They didn't know any better, but wanted to be accepted and approved of, so agreed to participate when they instinctively knew it didn't feel right. Women never want to feel as if they are simply a vehicle for a man to take his pleasure in. That is one of the worst experiences they can ever endure.

A man has to put enough attention on a woman for her to trust he wants to connect with her and not just have sex with her. Women want to feel men genuinely enjoy their company. It's the only thing that makes it feel safe for them. When it's safe they can allow themselves to have fun. They can enjoy the many delightful forms of foreplay, like kissing, cuddling, laughing and having sweet nothings whispered in their ear. This is the first and most important step to having the 'in the bedroom' connection - the sexual connection.

Women need to have their survival issues handled before they can be interested in sex. Sex may be momentary relief for a woman, but it won't be the quality of sex she's capable of having until she knows her survival issues are handled. A woman needs a roof over her head, the rent or mortgage handled, a reliable car to drive, food in the fridge, the phone bills covered, and a bit of cash for the unknowns, in order to be relaxed. Having her needs met will free her up to be fully present and deliciously available to her man.

A man who wants to have sex with a woman in survival is being insensitive to her. He is not paying close enough attention if he can't see she's struggling. When she is in survival, it would behoove a man to offer her financial assistance. Many times women are not willing to accept this kind of assistance from men because it means having to give up their story of woe. Some women enjoy being a victim on some level. If this is the case, he needs to move up to category #1 to reconnect with her and gain her trust.

If a woman is just dating a man it's not his job to pay her bills. However, he needs to be aware of the financial stress she may have in her life. He may think she is with him when they are together, but if she hasn't handled this month's bills, her attention will be divided.

Women feel safe when men are concerned about their needs. A man needs to be aware of the positive affect he can have on a woman when he is sensitive to her needs. Showing this kind of sensitivity will comfort her. When a woman knows she's not alone in the world and her man is there in supportive ways her confidence will be strengthened. A woman can become quite fearful when she's alone without support. She's not asking him to fix her problems. When a woman feels confident she becomes very creative .By lending a sympathetic ear, a man will prove to be a sensitive caring person. This kind of man is what every woman is looking for.

Women are much more fun to be with when their money situation is handled. If a man were to look for ways to contribute to the well-being of his woman he would receive major approval. It would be a loving, generous and caring act to offer assistance, knowing she is capable of taking care of herself, but seeing that her current situation needs support. She would love this kind of support. This would make her feel comfortable if she needed to ask for his help in the future. It means everything to a woman to have someone in the world she knows she can count on when the going gets rough.

I see many women driving around in Mercedes and BMWs. One would think they would be happy driving these luxurious machines. Not always true. If there is no connection with their man, fancy cars, fine homes, and closets full of clothes will never make them happy. Open and honest communication is what will buy a woman's happiness. It will put the smile on her face that a man is longing to see and won't cost a penny.

Men go broke trying to make women happy with baubles. Baubles are not necessary to a woman's survival – they are simply fun to have. They include jewelry, trips, flowers, fancy dinners, etc. Men can spend money buying women baubles day and night and never make them happy. It's demeaning to a woman when a man thinks he can buy her love and adoration. They love the gifts and attention, but not if the first two categories - connection and survival have not been tended to.

What makes a woman happy is having a man she can talk to. It's a man who listens to her and cares about the things that matter most to her. It's also a man who will hold her in his arms and let her know he'll always be there for her. It's a man who does what he says he's going to do. It's a huge plus for a woman to have a man who is willing to do all these things to satiate her needs. This is worth more than all the baubles she could have.

If a man's attention is on the category called 'baubles', which is her lowest priority, and she is not happy, he needs to move up one level to the 'food' category. If she's still not happy, it's because the most important category, the 'connection' category, has not been satisfied.

Trips are fun and can be romantic too. But have you ever noticed how exhausted you were upon returning from a vacation with your partner? You feel you need to take a separate vacation to recuperate. This is because trips are never a substitute or band-aid for communications that have gone unspoken and are long overdue. There's nothing like a good old-fashioned conversation on the couch to get connected again. If you think a vacation is going to be the cure-all for weeks of no connection, there is another thing to learn about a woman's priorities.

♂♀

It never goes over well for a man to give a woman flowers instead of a verbal apology for canceling a date. The verbal communication of an apology should always be your first choice. Flowers second. If a woman doesn't feel a sincere apology, she will know the man doesn't realize the impact of what he did. She'll suspect he will do it again which will decrease her level of trust for him. Sending flowers won't honor the true needs of a woman. Communicating honestly will.

Joy
is an
experience
that is
above
gratification.

Attributed to
Victor Baranco, Ph.D

Chapter 23

Present and Great Lovers

When all is said and done, to be a great lover has more to do with one's ability to be present than with any talent or acquired skill. When sex becomes a skill or a technique it creates distance instead of connection. The key is to enjoy the precious moments of NOW. The great lovers of the world understand that bringing their body, mind and spirit to the moment is what makes their love making a completely delicious experience. They know how to feel the sweetness of the moment and choose to enjoy it to the fullest.

When was the last time you focused on what truly pleases you? Do you give yourself permission to be pleasured in your daily life? What kind of priority have you given pleasure in your life? Our lives have become so hectic and stressful that we leave the possibility of pleasure for the end of the day when we're too tired. Many times pleasure ends up at the bottom of the priority list. Has your 'pleasure' muscle gone flabby and flat? What are you waiting for? If you aren't committed to your own pleasure who will be?

The great thing about being committed to your OWN pleasure, is that it gives you access to be present. I had a delightful discovery many years ago. I realized when I committed my life to being filled with pleasurable experiences, I was immediately more present to everything that surrounded me. *I had to be more present to know what my pleasure was.* This was a major 'ah ha' for me! I was able to utilize my senses in ways I was previously unaware of.

This discovery turned my sex life into a sensual life overnight. It's so much easier to enjoy whatever you are doing when you orient yourself around what pleases you. I became a 'piggy for pleasure' and started having much more fun. I started looking for what pleasured me in every situation. This instantly made me a lot more attractive to the opposite sex. By focusing on what pleasured me, I became a lot happier, and found men in my life winning much easier with me.

You are the one living inside your body. It would make sense that you would be the only one to know what makes it feel good. Many times when two people are touching their focus is on how to make the 'other' person feel good. They're in their head trying to figure out what their partner likes. They want to do it right because they want to please their partner. How can anyone really know what feels good to another person? They're not in that other person's body. The only thing anyone can know for sure is how their own body feels to them.

If it feels good to you, it will feel good to your partner. When you learn to focus your attention on your own pleasure, you'll be pleasantly surprised how quickly your partner will be pleasured as well. Whether it's your hands, your lips, or your whole body, focus on making it feel good to yourself, and it will instantly feel good to your partner. It's that simple. Being committed to making it feel good to you, forces you to be in present time. Touching someone when you are present to your pleasure will always feel good to the other person. You don't touch velvet for the sake of the velvet. You touch it to make it feel good to your hand.

There are quite a number of women who have a difficult time letting themselves fully enjoy the act of making love. They're unable to relax as easily as men. One of the reasons for their apprehension is that women don't trust that men are enjoying foreplay with them. If men are not verbalizing their enjoyment, women think they're simply going through the motions to get to the 'goal'.

It takes women longer to reach higher levels of pleasure. If women think they are taking too much time to achieve their pleasure, they will feel guilty. Women have many different frequencies on their 'guilt button', but every woman has one. Ideally, men want women to be fully present to the pleasure she's receiving and not in her head feeling guilty. When a man lets his woman know how much he enjoys being with her, it keeps the guilt button from going off the scale.

A good lover is someone who loves to do exactly what they're doing. When you love who you're with and what you're doing, you will have graduated from the Good Lover Hall of Fame. To get your diploma from GLHF, Lesson #1 is don't do anything you don't want to do. However, if you change your mind, make sure you do whatever you decide to do with enjoyment and gusto. You can turn any negative situation around in an instant. Just be present to the moment, and put your attention on what you love. This is the simplest and most powerful key to enjoying yourself and becoming a great lover.

A woman relaxes when a man genuinely enjoys her. She loves when a man verbally acknowledges that he's pleasured by what he sees and what he's touching. When a man enjoys what he's doing with his woman, and gives her lots of verbal appreciation, a woman can surrender more easily to her pleasure. Women would be able to enjoy a lot more of their intimate life if men would express their pleasure in being with them more often. A man can never say too much about how he enjoys his woman. She can never receive enough adoration about her body. Women love it when men are specific in what they notice - the softness of their skin, how great their hair smells or how delicious they taste. Even more enjoyment happens when men express their pleasure by making their manly moans and sighs. This may be embarrassing at first but it's quite a turn on for a woman. It will not only enhance his own turn on, it will make her enjoy him even more.

♂♀

The best sex is sex women want. Imagine a world where men controlled the sexual activity on the planet. We would never get any work done, that's for sure. We would have sex all the time and would quickly create an overpopulated planet. It would be a woman's worst nightmare. Thankfully, women are in charge of this arena. However, society hasn't convinced men of this yet. Most women haven't realized that a man's sex life is dependant on her appetite.

The only sex worth having is when a woman is turned on and truly desires it. Men would do much better in their relationships with women if they would accept this. Many women resent having to perform sex simply because their man demands it. It is one of the most damaging things that can happen in relationships. To act as if it's a woman's job to please a man is definitely an attitude of the dark ages. This is a huge no no.

Sadly, many women have been programmed to take care of their man's sexual needs morning, noon, and night, regardless of their own desire. The truth is, women don't want sex as much as men do. Think about how many cows are put in a pasture with one bull. Sometimes dozens! That's because one bull can carry on till the cows come home. He may not get to all the cows but the females won't be crying over spilled milk.

Too many times a woman has sex in order to please her man. Women have sex for social reasons; his birthday, their anniversary, he's going away on a business trip, or just returned from one. She will have sex with him because she feels it's her duty.

Women don't want it simply because a man does. Women will torture their man in subtle ways if they think they have to please him against their will. Sex is never satisfying when it happens without a woman's desire. Like everything else in a woman's world, she only wants it when she wants it.

A woman's heart and soul has to be included in making love or she won't be making love, she'll be making trouble. It is rarely satisfying for a woman when she has sex out of obligation. She will be in her head just going through the motions. She will plan some small revenge because she will be upset with herself for selling out one more time.

It's not that women don't want sex. They just want sex they desire. Men can make women feel safer by letting them know he's aware that she's in charge. She will then be able to trust him. Trust and safety are necessary keys to a woman's sexual desire.

Sexual desire is the essence of a woman. Her sexual appetite and desire is the most powerful force in the world. This force is what creates life on earth. It creates the propagation of our species. By honoring women for their desire and timing, men are honoring their true essence.

The
Joy of
a Woman
is
Loving
Her.

*Attributed to
Victor Baranco, Ph.D*

Chapter 24

The True Power of a Woman

Women are waking up to the incredible power they have. They are beginning to learn how to use it to their advantage. It appears to society that men are the ones in the position of power. Nothing could be further from the truth. Women are the ones who are actually in the driver's seat. Unfortunately, most of their driving has been on the wrong side of the street.

Women need to allow themselves to utilize more of their feminine side. The sweet, kind and playful aspects of a woman need to be present in their everyday lives. These qualities have been suppressed for too long. As soon as women learn to put attention on these vitally important characteristics everyone will benefit. The man-woman dynamic will become more balanced when women return to their feminine essence.

Feminine power can get a man's attention any time day or night. It's more natural for women to use their femininity than it is for them to use the masculine aspects of power they've been using. Acting like a man not only takes more effort, it causes an imbalance between men and women. Women have taken on a few too many masculine traits and, unfortunately, have not seen how unattractive this is to men. If women would use more of their femininity they would be more attractive and less intimidating.

♂ ♀

Women match men on many academic levels and have proven to equal the best of them. Becoming equal to men in the academic world has been necessary for the advancement of a woman's status. Women are smart, many times much smarter than men, because of their intuition. A woman's true power comes from her femininity, however, not her intellect. Her feminine power gives her access to a higher state of awareness. Women use their intuition and senses as well as their intelligence. The more a woman utilizes the gift of her senses and feminine side, the softer and more powerful she becomes. The world needs women to exercise their 'soft' muscles. 'Smart' muscles are good, but 'soft' muscles are better.

Being soft and vulnerable is attractive to a man. It will get a woman everything she wants. Women who are willing to be feminine are incredibly attractive to men. They are receptive, open, soft and vulnerable. This kind of behavior is an automatic invitation for any man to step up to the plate and use his manliness to forward her goals. When a woman is vulnerable, a man's natural instinct is to protect her. He is ready, willing and able, to do whatever he can to make her feel safe, happy and fulfilled. He will get to be the manly producer and provider. In turn, she gets to have all her needs met.

Women have avoided being soft and vulnerable because they have been told to be soft, is to lose their power. They've needed to be tough to make it in today's world - a world run mostly by men. Sadly, this has been a world where most men have not been awake enough to know how to empower women. Whether a man is awake or not, there's always one thing that will get his attention every time - a woman who's soft, real and vulnerable. This is the essence of a woman and where she finds her power. Soft is good. Vulnerable is precious. And real is an absolute must.

Are you smart, delicious, or both? We know what it means to be smart. What does it mean to be delicious? A delicious woman is one who is in touch with her femininity and sensuality. It's a way to express and exude the essence of womanhood. Many women are unbalanced and push themselves too hard to be successful. They have forgotten to include their femininity. When women learn to balance their femininity with their intelligence, they will be recognized as truly powerful women. They will be women who have the kind of confidence that is refreshingly feminine. This balance will empower her to make the incredible contributions that only intelligent, feminine women can make.

♂♀

Men feel good about themselves when they're with women who are adorable. To adore a woman is to worship her, admire her, respect her, and be passionate about her - to love her unconditionally. Men would love to see adorable women on every corner. It would inspire them to be the sexy knight in shining armor they always dream of being. Whenever a man comes across a woman in trouble, a damsel in distress he will jump at the opportunity to save her. When a woman's in distress, she will let her guard down and become vulnerable. This becomes an automatic opening for a man to rescue her. Women should let themselves be rescued more often.

Women love to be adored by men. They don't know that their un-adorable behavior prevents this from happening. They don't realize that adorable means to be sweet, delightful, charming, attractive and lovable. Deep down every woman melts when a man adores her.

Women are confused about where the men have gone. It's simple. They haven't been adorable and men are only attracted to women who have traits of being adorable. Remember, the words that describe adorable have nothing to do with pretty, and everything to do with attitude. Sweet, lovable, endearing and delightful - that's adorable. There's nothing weak about adorable.

Adorable women are hard to find but easy to recognize. They're the ones who are having the best time. They're delighted and interested in everything around them. They're having fun because they make it fun. They like themselves enough to put their attention on things outside of themselves. They're attractive to others because they make others feel good. They're happy with however things go in every moment. They have no agenda. They simply go with the flow and interact with the world in a playful way. They are a magnet for any kind of fun!

A man's natural response to an adorable woman is to move toward her. Men are like weather vanes. A weather vane doesn't think about what direction it moves, it simply moves when the wind changes. Men do the same when it comes to responding to anything or anyone that's fun. They are on automatic pilot looking for opportunities to play, especially if an adorable woman is involved. If she's being adorable she's exposing sides of herself that are always endearing to a man. Every time a woman chooses adorable over not so adorable, she's invites fun into both their lives.

Learning to be playful is one of the most important things a woman could learn from this book. Many women who have reached positions of power, have often done so by controlling and manipulating their circumstances. They thought this was the only way to achieve their success. It has not occurred to women they could also reach these levels of success without being controlling. They adopted this mode of operating without seeing the negative effect it had on the dynamics of man-woman. Women haven't known they could accomplish the same result, and more powerfully, by using their feminine nature.

Controlling women are not feminine women. Men always want to steer away from controlling women. Women could radically transform everything they touch if they shifted their controlling mode of operating to one of care and compassion. Women are in charge of many aspects of relating, however, they need to stop steering the direction of things with their masculine side. This mode of operating is unnecessary for their success and usually backfires where no one ends up getting what they want. When women finally choose to allow their feminine side to run the show, they will begin to attract exactly what they want easily and effortlessly.

Magic happens when women play instead of control. It's natural for women to play, but they usually reserve their playful behavior for other women in their life. We all know that girls just want to have fun. Women need to direct some of that fun towards men. Men want to have fun too. It's the catalyst for them to produce beyond a woman's wildest dreams. Men will do whatever they can to assist women to get what they want if a woman's attitude is playful and positive, instead of controlling.

♂♀

The act of kindness is never wasted. No matter how small a gesture, it is the gift that keeps on giving in any relationship. Whether it's thanking your postman for delivering your mail or letting someone in line ahead of you at the grocery store, kindness matters. Being kind is being caring, thoughtful and compassionate. It takes a kind and loving heart to have a woman experience being tender, soft and playful. We must never underestimate the power of exercising the 'kindness' muscle.

If males
had the
answer,
there wouldn't
be females.

Attributed to
Victor Baranco, Ph.D

Chapter 25

Turning a Nightmare into a Dream

One of the quickest ways for a man to put a halt to a new and budding relationship is to have an agenda. Not every man has an agenda. An agenda can be an admirable way to achieve certain results. However, hidden agendas do not sit well with women, especially if it's a man's sexual agenda. Men who have sexual agendas don't realize how much it prevents them from getting what they want. Men will win more with women as soon as they give up their agendas. They would be better off hoping for sex, than expecting it. The smart man will figure out what her agenda is.

Women need to enlighten men, in a nice way, that their sexual agenda won't work. Women lose the ability to trust men when they sense they have an agenda. If a woman doesn't trust her man, it's next to impossible to find the desire to make love to him. It makes a woman uneasy to think that the only reason he is interested in her is for his sexual gratification. When a man has an agenda that supersedes a woman's desire, she cannot help feeling apprehensive. She knows he's not being sensitive to her needs which makes her feel unsafe.

Women are sensitive to a man's agenda - they can't be fooled. She knows when he's busy thinking of ways to get her into bed. It makes her feel uneasy. An automatic response when she senses a man's sexual agenda is to shut down. It's not wrong for men to have an agenda - it just gets in the way. Their agenda won't produce satisfying results. They create more separation than connection.

Women complain about men being so focused on sex and don't realize it's simply the nature of what it means to be a man. The essence of a woman is sensual - the nature of a man is sexual. A women's appetite for sex is not as constant as a man's and can change as often as the weather. Thank heavens men want sex all the time because their drive for it increases the odds of making it happen.

Throughout this book I mention over and over how much a woman loves a man's attention. When a man honors what her attention is on, and reacts appropriately, he will always win. He will earn her respect when he follows her lead. Following a woman's lead tells her that he knows she's steering the relationship. This empowers her to direct it toward the fun they both want. This is how a man becomes more attractive to a woman. The more a man honors her the more she will reciprocate in kind and loving ways.

A man's agenda is not the problem, it's his attachment to his agenda. Many times the mood will quickly change as soon as the man realizes there will be no nookie tonight. This will leave the woman feeling unwanted. It will be clear to her that he won't enjoy being with her without the possibility of sex. Men have a bad reputation for this. Women are disgusted when men want them only for their sexual gratification. This will turn a woman off more than anything. Do men really think women want to get into bed with them, without being friends first? This kind of behavior causes women to be more on guard with men. Most women aren't interested in sex for the sake of sex, they want the heart connection first.

If a man wants to make love with a woman, it has to be on her terms. This is where patience is an important virtue for men. If he is willing to be patient and learns to enjoy the other aspects of her, he will be pleased with how she responds. This will make her more willing to entertain his sexual advances.

Men fear they won't get their needs met - the opposite is true. Women want men to have what they want too. Women have an amazing capacity to satisfy and enrich a man's life. Nothing would make them happier than to have their man be completely fulfilled as well. However, women will shut down and go away if they think a man is attached to having his needs met first. His menacing attachment to his sexual agenda simply needs to be revered as a goal whose time has ended.

A woman's ability to attract a man is thwarted when he is attached to his agenda. Women must be acknowledged for their feminine power of attraction. This power belongs only to women. She needs to be recognized for her gift of being able to turn a man's head whenever she wants. If a man thinks he's in charge of attracting a woman he is dead wrong. When a woman meets a man who thinks he's in charge of the turn on, she becomes turned off by his ignorance. Sometimes it is actually better for a woman to be without a man, than to be with one who thinks he runs the show.

Women know men want sex. Women want it too. But women only want it when they truly desire it. Men have to keep in mind that women want to connect sexually, however, their desire for it is not as rampant as a man's.

Women love the feeling of oneness that only two lovers wrapped up in the moment can have. This experience of being totally connected and lost in bliss is vitally important to a woman. If, however, sex is forced on her in anyway, subtle or not so subtle, it's the beginning of the end of any genuine connection.

Man-woman relationships have been in trouble mainly because a woman's wants and desires have not been the top priority. If women simply had their needs met, it would make the biggest difference to the success of relationships. The trouble is, men haven't been taught to focus on a woman's priorities first.

Women would love to create more fun in their lives, but they too, haven't known how vital it is for their needs be a priority. The opportunity for women to be more fun is created when she is simply honored and accepted for what she wants.

A woman feels respected, regarded and known when a man appreciates her for all her feminine qualities. Women rarely feel appreciated by men at this level. This kind of acknowledgment gives women room to be the feminine creature they are. There's nothing better for a woman than to be with a man who makes her feel this way. "Ladies first" is a good motto for men to adopt in any interaction they have with women.

♂♀

Women think that who they are and what they have to say is more interesting than anything a man could conjure up. They can't understand why men are not too interested in knowing the details of the world of women. Women don't realize the things that make men happy are a lot simpler than the things that make a complex woman happy.

When I think of the picture of the control panels of men versus women, I am reminded of the many different buttons, levers and dials it takes to operate a woman. Each one of those precious buttons can open up a whole new world for a man. If a man were to honor and appreciate all her buttons and tune in to the frequency she's vibing at, a woman would joyfully invite him into her world. Joining his masculine world with her feminine world will enhance his life in ways he could only dream of. His production would be inspired tenfold. Give a woman an inch of respect and she will give you a mile.

The old saying, "Behind every great man, is a great woman", could be expanded to include, "He was empowered and inspired by her because he had high regard for her." Behind every great man is a great woman who he values and admires. In return she would shower him with her love and positive feminine energy. This would give him the most powerful energy on the planet - her feminine energy. With this energy he knows there is nothing he couldn't accomplish. She would be able to steer him in ways that would empower him to produce on a grand scale. This would be the result of a man's conscious decision to allow his woman to live in her place of power.

Being
ruthless
in the
pursuit of
pleasure is
commendable.

Attributed to
Victor Baranco, Ph.D

Chapter 26

Everything Matters

My father taught me the importance of appreciating the simple things in life. When you pay attention to the details in life, you can breathe life into whatever you touch. I watched him hose off our entire driveway on many weekends. It was never really dirty but it always made a wonderful difference to the space around our home. He always quoted the well-known adage, "Cleanliness is next to Godliness." It was my father's influence of cleanliness and impeccability that had me grow up to appreciate how much a conscious environment mattered. When I pay attention to details of my own environment and have them exactly the way I want them, it gives me a sense of freedom and more space to be creative. I feel nourished by what I've chosen to have around me.

Everything you have in your home has it's own energy. If it's in your space, you will be affected by it on an energetic level. The question is, how is your environment affecting you? Does it make you feel positive when you walk in the door or negative? Or do you even think it matters? Everything about you and your environment communicates something.

You may be thinking, what does this have to do with man-woman relationships? It has everything to do with it because everything around you is an extension of who you are. Whether we think it matters or not it is irrelevant. Your environment is always communicating the level of good you are willing to have in your life and how much you respect and love yourself. When you love yourself, you realize that everything around you is a reflection of that love. Your car, your bedroom, your body, your office all communicates how much you matter to you. Is your world clean, orderly and conscious? Do you take care of it so it can take care of you? Do you respect your possessions and treat them accordingly?

Men and women greatly benefit when they care about how they present themselves. The first thing people do when they meet someone is size them up by their physical appearance. When you care enough about yourself, the person you want to impress will notice. It's obvious to a woman that if a man doesn't care about his clothes being presentable he probably has the same set of standards for his car and home. It's a red flag for a woman when a man's car is not clean and conscious.

Women don't want to have their attention on this area of a man's life. A woman will have a tendency to want to mother him about things if he hasn't handled them himself. We all know 'mothering women' can cause the magic in a relationship to disappear. When a man pays attention to his appearance, it communicates to her that he likes himself enough to look his best. Women like it when men care about their bodies and their surroundings. They know if he puts this kind of attention on his own environment he will be more likely to give her the same quality of attention.

Men need to know how much the little things mean to women. There is a myth in the world that women are expensive to keep. I am not saying this isn't true but a more accurate truth is, the things that mean the most to a woman don't cost money. It's the little things that count. A flower he picks from his garden, a note he writes for no special reason, or an e-mail he sends about how special she is. These are the simple things that mean the most to her.

An old boyfriend of mine once spent all afternoon making a precious valentine card out of a manila file folder. He cut it into a heart and then wrote the most touching poem anyone had ever written for me. The poem captured our relationship from the moment we met on the dance floor one year earlier to the present. It was simple, pure and straight from his heart. This meant more to me than anything he could have ever bought me. All the special moments of our relationship were highlighted in that poem. The fact that he remembered these in such a precious way, affected me in a delicious way every time I looked at it.

♂♀

The bedroom needs to be inviting. The place in people's homes that usually need the most attention is their bedroom. If you put attention on this room alone, your sensual life will transform over night. Think about the possibility of being turned on the minute you open your bedroom door. Feel the welcoming and sensual space you've created by putting attention on every detail. This room could be a great source of pleasure for you, even when you are alone. If you are turned on being in this inviting space, imagine how your partner will feel.

You can address your sense of smell with aroma therapy candles, incense or fresh flowers. Your sense of touch could be enhanced with Egyptian cotton sheets, a chenille throw or a feather. The whole ambiance could be improved by adding a sound system to play your favorite music that inspires you. To tantalize your taste buds, you could have that heirloom dish filled with chocolates or strawberries and a special glass filled with your favorite drink. Last but not least, the visual appearance of your room could be transformed in a delicious way with your favorite comforter, several posh pillows, fresh flowers on your dresser, and everything in its place. The key to a more sensual life is having your bedroom nurture and enliven you the minute you walk in the door.

♂ ♀

Practice good Feng Shui and more good will come your way. Feng Shui is the ancient Chinese art of placement that brings harmony and balance to your life through your environment. I had my home Feng Shui'd several years ago and continue to notice the healing and nurturing benefits every day. It is lively, energizing, peaceful and precious. I feel loved by everything around me and when people walk into my home, the first thing they notice is how comfortable and welcoming it feels. They notice that everything is deliberately placed in a way that obviously matters. It makes every nook and cranny more inviting. It's appealing to people because they feel everything is placed deliberately with love and consciousness.

Living in a space that is nourishing to your soul will keep you centered and grounded. Your well-being has a positive affect on your ability to manifest more of what you want. The only world you can immediately impact is the world directly in front of you. Start by opening your eyes and notice everything that surrounds you. Apply the idea that everything matters in your environment, and you will be living in a world with more peace, balance and harmony. A new level of energy will pervade every moment. You will be more awake and available to receive all the blessings that are your birthright.

The gifts of life are in the simple things. If you find yourself searching for more meaning and purpose in your life, it is because you need to simplify your life. You need to stop and "smell the roses". How many people take the time to enjoy the simple things that affect their senses? Do you take time to watch a humming bird, to listen to your favorite music, to feel the breeze on your skin, to consciously taste a piece of fresh fruit or to smell the ocean air? Do you ever take time to simply enjoy what you've worked so hard to create? If not, perhaps you need to start enjoying the fruits of your labor right now. We are usually too busy living for the future instead of being present to the gifts of the moment.

The more you notice, the more there is to enjoy. To enjoy the simple things in life you must be awake and conscious enough to notice them. A simple, mindful action that will produce profound results is when you learn to use your 'awareness' muscle. Begin to make it a daily priority to pay attention to everything around you. You use your senses all the time but haven't been using them to your advantage.

Slow down, and get in present time, and you will begin to notice things you never could before. You can't see the forest for the trees if you are going 90 miles an hour through your life. The more time you take to notice the details of your life, the more you will experience the simpler joys life has to offer.

Pay attention to detail and it will open up a whole new world. Women probably pay more attention to detail than men, because they are multi-tasked and are capable of putting attention on many things at the same time. There is something very sexy, however, about a man who has an appreciation for details. It's the little things that mean the most to women and when a man notices specific things about her, it alters the quality of their relating. When men and women pay attention to the world around them, there will be more to share and experience with each other.

You will have a much richer life when you become an observer of the world around you. If you are willing to put your attention on something outside of yourself, people will find you more fun to be around. You will wake people up and show them how much more there is to life. We have all been missing the real blessings of life that are everywhere to be found, by not enjoying the simple things.

♂♀

Everyone needs to learn, sooner or later, that you are the one who matters most. Look around. Do you think anyone else is concerned about your life more than you? Everyone has their attention on their life. You are the one who should be focusing on your life first. This is not selfish. This is necessary because you and only you, know what's best for you.

Give yourself permission - if you don't who will? Giving yourself permission to put your attention on yourself first is probably one of the more difficult challenges you have to overcome. So many of us think that we will matter more by taking care of others first. But if you are waiting for somebody else to give you the experience that you matter, you may be waiting for quite some time. Your life is not a top priority to them.

Taking care of yourself first will nourish everyone else in your life. It's not that people don't care, but people don't have the capacity to care for those outside themselves, until they learn to care for themselves. Caring for yourself means, not taking on other people's problems until your own spirit is nourished. Surround yourself with things that make your heart sing. When you are happy inside and out, you become more capable of contributing in a positive way to everything around you. Have your body, mind and spirit soar first and others will be inspired to follow.

Honor yourself in all areas of your life, because YOU matter! When you understand there is no one in the world who can live your life as perfectly as you, you have learned to honor and accept who you are. If you accept yourself, you will be able to accept everyone else as well. When you matter the most, you attract people of like mind. Life begins to unfold in ways that are precious, uplifting and magical. You will find joy and laughter in all that you do.

PART
II

The
Man-Woman
Course

Clearly Related

2002

San Francisco

Welcome to the Clearly Related Course. This course originated from a weekend seminar I took in 1985. I had a major epiphany when I heard this information and was blown away by the clarity, the simplicity and the dynamic of the whole message. I was thirty-six years old at the time and totally amazed that I had never heard any of these man-woman distinctions. I knew if I didn't know this, chances were pretty good that few of my sisters on the planet did, either.

For the first time in my life, I finally understood why none of my relationships ever worked. I didn't understand who I was really dealing with in the opposite sex. I didn't understand the nature of men. When you discover what I learned and want to show you, it will surprise and amaze you, I promise. It will immediately change your relationship with your husband, your wife, your boyfriend or your girlfriend.

You always hear women say 'men are so dumb', for not understanding women. When women make these kinds of statements, they are putting men at fault for being the way they are. Men really are uninformed about women. Once you discover this truth, you'll see that the man-woman game is a perfect dynamic. It's not about right or wrong. It's about understanding how this beautiful game works for both sexes and how incredibly powerful it can be.

God created men and women, to be together in a most extraordinary way. What's the problem? We never took Relationships 101. God didn't make a mistake when he created us so different; we just never got the handbook on who we're really dealing with in the opposite sex.

My religion is very simple. My religion is kindness.
Dalai Lama

Look at the mess relationships are in today. In most case people are not connected where it counts. We haven't figured out what is most dear to us - our man-woman relationships. Our relationship with our self is one of the keys to successful relating and is totally necessary for an extraordinary relationships with the opposite sex.

A lot of us keep telling ourselves we've had too many failed relationships, "there must be something wrong with me." Don't run the 'I am wrong' number on yourselves, because you will discover later on that it's one of the most unattractive things you do to yourself. When you think you're wrong, don't look to someone else to fix it. Men certainly don't have any idea how to fix you. He'll look over at you, a broken woman, and think, 'Uh-oh, big problem here. I'm not going to be able to fix this.' So what does he do? He watches more sports, works longer hours, or goes to the bar with the guys.

Please don't play the blame game. You may think, at some point during this course that you have been wrong, because you'll see things that you did in the past without knowing the effect it would have. You might say, 'Oh my God, I did those things to my last boyfriend. But this conversation is not about blaming anyone, especially yourself.

I want you to imagine two separate boxes. Imagine they're the kind of electronic boxes you've seen a hundred times in electronic stores, except there's something very different with these boxes. On one of the boxes there's only

---

Life is what happens when you are making other plans.
John Lennon

one switch, it's a toggle switch. The word at the top of this box says MAN and the words above and below the switch say ON and OFF.

The other box is a lot more complicated. At first glance it seems to have hundreds of buttons, levers and dials; many with different colors and sizes. Each dial is important and has a different function. In order for this box to operate at it's maximum efficiency each button, lever and dial has to be there. The word at the top of this box says WOMAN.

Imagine that the toggle switch on the MAN box is ON. That'll be easy to do, because men are always on. They are ready and willing. Now imagine all the dials on the WOMAN box are accepted exactly the way they are. This would guarantee the easiest and the best way to operate the players in the man-woman dynamic.

One of the most important elements of a long lasting and intimate man-woman relationship is understanding and celebrating our unique differences.

You're going to learn how to get your partner to love your dials just the way they are. If you look at the possibility of what these dials are really saying, you'll discover something amazing. You'll discover a refreshingly new paradigm that will enable you to understand and communicate in a much easier way with the opposite sex.

Men always want to be a woman's first love; women like to be a man's last romance.   Oscar Wilde

This is the reality of the way it's always been, that hasn't been embraced until now. For men who can tune electronic equipment pretty easily, this one called woman, boggles their minds. This is the real world, the way it is in with woman that men have to learn how to deal with. And we wonder why communication between the sexes is so difficult.

If a man had to experience the energy of a woman in the middle of her heat cycle, they'd have to put him in a straitjacket. He would not know how to deal with all the erratic feminine energy. Women are out of their bodies a lot of time but always see and feel everything that's going on around them.

Guy's faces are rather expressionless compared to women. They are just hanging out doing what's in front of them. Women, however, have a zillion things going on and whatever they feel is written all over their face. This is how it is for women. And we wonder why men are intimated by us. They can't understand us and definitely can't control us.

We're going to talk about operating from 'what a woman wants', because she is all about desire. All those buttons, levers, and dials are about different things women desire.

You'll discover this truth by observing it in your own life. Guys are pretty steady-state. Women are much more interested in how it feels right now and men are much more interested in their goals of the future.

The best work we can all do is to create the highest vision possible for our lives and be led by that vision to the greatest good.   Oprah

Men are result oriented and women are present time oriented. If women are having a good time right now, we don't care when we get to the goal. We don't care if we get to the 'Big O', either. If we're not having a good time now, we won't get to the 'Big O' - it's as simple as that. If it's fun now, we want more. If it's not, we're done!

This is not to say men are insensitive. They are super sensitive. As a matter of fact, they're much more sensitive than a lot of women realize. They just manage their senses in a different way. What women have done is shut men down. We have been ruthlessly unkind in certain ways, not because we necessarily intended to, but mostly because we don't understand men. The attacks they've gotten from us have hurt so much, they've had to shut down and put their walls up. They've been attacked because we didn't know how to relate to them in a way that inspired them to want to do for us. Instead, women got the old crowbar out. The crowbar, the manipulation, the threats, and all the stuff we do, is not wrong. It was the only way women knew to get their needs met. Everybody knows if a woman's needs aren't met, she won't be a very fun person to be around. 'If Mama ain't happy, nobody's happy.'

So I invite you to keep an open mind and see how these ideas fit. We're not doing the 'victim' thing here. If you feel somebody's done something to you and you feel victimized, then what you've actually done is given your power away. People just do what they do. You choose how you want to feel about it. People don't make you feel a particular way. You make yourself feel all the ways that you do. Everybody is 100% responsible for their experience in life. Things just

Nobody can make you feel inferior without your permission.
Eleanor Roosevelt

happen. Life is 10% what happens to you and 90% what you do with it. You can choose to be a victim or you can choose victory over whatever happens.

♂♀

This is not a get-well conversation. When you play the get-well game, you're always trying to 'fix the bad'. And if you put your attention all day long on fixing 'the bad', by the end of the day, you'll have 'bad' all around you. Whatever you put your attention on expands. This conversation is about expanding the 'good' in your life. Having the 'good' get better. It's about celebrating what you already have in life. When you come from this place you'll end up having more of what you really want.

This is not some kind of game. This is about honest and truthful relating from the heart. No one likes to play games. However, there is a dynamic present whenever a man and a woman are together and choose to relate over something. There's a way you can interact with each other that is much more uplifting. It's more fun, it's cleaner and it honors both of the sexes. It's a dynamic that most people in the world are not aware of. This conversation is about the quality of relating, not the form. I'm not attached to the form. I don't think people should be married.

I have a relationship of extraordinary quality with my former husband, John. We've known each other twenty years. We were together for three years, then we weren't together for three years. When we were apart, I met a group of people and discovered what real relating was all about. When I saw him after three years of separation, I had learned my craft

What you wish to experience, provide for another.
Dalai Lama

as a woman in relationship to men. Knowing this made it easy to win him back. The reason he didn't like being with me the first time we were together was because I didn't take responsibility for my role in why the relationship wasn't working. I wouldn't own it. I kept pointing my finger at him. But when I figured this out, all of a sudden I realized, "Oh my God, there's three fingers pointing back at me." That's when I discovered my power. I saw for the first time, how much of an effect I had on men.

John asked me to marry him when he knew I realized how much I was responsible for the way the relationship would go. We flew to Las Vegas, got married, and then decided to further our studies at an institute in Northern California. They had been researching and studying the man-woman dynamic for the past several decades.

We soon discovered what few people know about man-woman. We learned a unique and powerful way of relating, real relating. We've been teaching it to the world ever since. The quality of our relationship is extraordinary. There is nothing we wouldn't do for each other. We came together for some very valuable lessons in life; the main one being how to love each other unconditionally. Even though I am no longer married to John, I love him completely. I even introduce him to girlfriends and other women I meet and have no jealousy around this. He knows about my male friends as well. We always celebrate each other's joy.

It's about the quality of our relating. Who cares about the form of the relationship, if the quality is a nightmare? When people think of the word "relationship" a lot of noise

---

*A woman's job is to speak into existence
the world she wants to have.   Edwene Gaines*

comes up because of all our failures. But relating with the opposite sex is a lot simpler when you focus on the quality rather than the form. That's what this conversation will produce for you - more quality in your relationships. It's easier to focus on the quality because the 'quality of life' is experienced in the now, not the future. It's about how it feels to relate with this person, now. The quality will be good when your attention is on having it feel good now. Living in the moment produces a whole lot more joy.

♂♀

Let me tell you about an extraordinary dancer whose name is Victor; a former boyfriend and a major friend of mine for life. I met him right before my fiftieth birthday. I was having a dance party and thought, "Okay, God, a babe like me should not be going to her fiftieth birthday without some yummy guy to dance with." I didn't have a man in my life at the time, so I went off to a dance club not far from my home. It happened to be a Latin dance night. I thought if he could dance Latin, he would be a sexy dancer.

Sure enough, 20 minutes later, this handsome man tapped me on the shoulder. As I turned around, he looked at me straight in the eye and offered his hand. I took his hand and he twirled me right into his arms. I love to dance. He spun me, dipped me and twirled me around for the next couple of hours. By the end of the night, I was doing five spins at a time, and at the end of every song he'd drop my head down to the floor. I decided to hand him my invitation and said, "You are definitely invited to my birthday dance party." He could not believe I was turning fifty. He thought I looked about thirty-eight. "Well, how old are you?" I asked.

Treat everyone you meet like God in drag.
Ram Dass

He looked to me like about thirty-six. Well, he was twenty-six. So here we had twenty-three years difference, but it didn't matter. I could tell from the moment I met him that he was a class act. I found out later he was a navy lieutenant.

Victor arrived at the party in his gorgeous military uniform and knocked the socks off every one of my girlfriends including my former 77 year-old mother in-law, who hadn't danced in twenty-two years. Victor danced with each woman as if there was no other woman on the planet.

We became wonderful friends. I think we made a deal somewhere up above before we were born, that when I was fifty, he would show up in my life. I would teach him all about man-woman, sex and sensuality, and he would dance me into a new chapter of my life. He gave me an extraordinary gift that allowed the little kid in me to come out and play. He liked to play and have fun and I loved to play with him.

I was able to experience so many new sides of myself with Victor because he never, in the entire two years we were together, judged me or made me wrong for anything. I had total permission to be all of the different women inside of me. I had the experience of being completely free. He did a wonderful thing for me by 'paying' attention". Do we hear that, guys? Yes. Pay attention! That was his gift—his extraordinary ability to simply be focused on whoever was in front of him.

One of the most important things to a woman is that her man pays quality attention to her. I was able to experience this quality with Victor because he was very willing to learn

---

Why postpone happiness?
Paramahansa Yogananda

everything he could about women. If you're not paying attention, you're going to miss a lot in life. You see, if you're really paying attention to a woman, she will experience the man as 'safe' for her. This is very important for women.

If men really pay quality attention to a woman and she experiences that it is safe for her, she will open up and allow the man to experience the many different sides of her. She will show men things she never would have, if she thought he was going to judge her. Women want to let the cats, all the different cats out of the bag to play. But unless they know that men will honor and not judge any of them, many of the cats will be off limits.

You see, women are already judging themselves madly and furiously about many things; good, bad, right, wrong. That's just what comes with the female package. Our bodies, the men in our life and our jobs. There is always something we're not satisfied with. We don't need men to judge us on top of what we are already judging. And if men do, they get big 'X s' from women, which is not what men are looking for. Men are looking for approval; the ' ✔ s' in life. The more ✔ s you get from a woman, the more she wants to open up and show you all her fun sides.

We want men to love, be enamored by, and adore all of those crazy wild women inside. Even the bitch! Actually, ladies, men love the bitch. They know it's there. They don't love it as the main item on the menu, but they know it's there and it doesn't deter them from pursuing us if it comes in small doses. Women are the ones who have a problem with

Would you like to see God's world or
are you happy with yours?   Unkown

213

that side of themselves. If we didn't have such a problem with it, it wouldn't be so horrible for the guys. An overt bitch, a woman who owns it, is more attractive than a covert bitch.

♂ ♀

The biological differences we have are not flaws. They're actually an incredible opportunity to relate with each other in a whole new way. There's a poster that reads, "Men and women are the same, just different." We are similar in that we are human beings. We are all spirits learning how to give love and receive love; men and women, the same.

Some of us were born in the pink pile and some of us in the blue pile. I want to take this conversation to a more basic level. It's all fine and dandy that we're spiritual beings and we want to be fully expressed creatures. The breakdowns happen when you wake up in the morning and you've got someone in the blue pile lying next to you and who hasn't paid attention to you for weeks. If you're the guy in the blue pile waking up to your darling in the pink pile, and she's still miffed at you - for you know not what you do? There are so many subtle, and not so subtle, ways that men and women end up disconnected from each other. Well, stay tuned, because we are going to shed some major light on this subject.

Basically, men want to know what their job is. What could they do? How could they win with you? The world of men is a much simpler world than that of women. I don't mean that in a demeaning way at all. It's just a much less complicated world for men than it is for women. And it's really perfect, because men have an amazing quality of being able

There are no final solutions – the dance changes every day.
Kristinaism

to focus; they get the job done! If they break a nail, it's no big deal. If a woman breaks a nail, it's, "Oh no, I can't believe it!" We have to stop immediately, get our nail fixed, and then get further distracted by saying, "Why don't we get a latte and go shopping because I heard Nordie's has a sale on." Women will do that. We'll fix the airplane later. We'll try to remember what screw we bolted down or what screw we didn't bolt down, but we'll handle it later because it doesn't look like fun right now. It's a good thing that men have a logical, linear ability to get the job done because they know how to go from A to Z without getting interrupted.

Women can do the same things guys can do, and most women will probably think they can do it faster and more efficiently. But what do they do? They get in there and do it all themselves. This is one of the breakdowns that happens out there in the world. When Gloria Steinem and the feminist movement emerged, we all decided, "We're going to show the guys that we don't need them. We can get it done without them." Complete focus is one of the things women can do. Like a laser, we get on something and can't be stopped. Well, it's all fine - we've done that. We've made it in a man's world. We have great careers and big salaries, but the result is, we've taken everything into our own hands. We've become 'women with dicks'. And how fun is that? Not very. It's not fun and it's definitely not attractive. We've become more male than female. We've become men.

We are multi-tasked creatures. We can do a zillion things at the same time and stay completely focused. You often see women driving down the freeway putting their eye makeup on in the mirror, drinking their latte, talking on their

It is the learning you have in the near future that is going to give you your next set of cards to play with. And a winner you will be in whatever game that turns out to be. T. Anchorman

cell phone and driving at the same time. Men on the other hand, will have their hands on the wheel and maybe their cell phone on, but they're not doing six different things at the same time. Not like they can't, but it's highly unlikely. It's a different world for men.

I'm simply drawing the distinctions and differences between the two sexes because without this understanding we miss the opportunity for romance. Without knowing this, the romance, the joy, the dance and the juice disappears. If women are running around doing it all themselves, how can a man be romantic? Where does he get to be the white knight? There is no opportunity for men to be our hero.

Many men think it's not fun to relate with us because they don't feel needed. Women have made it in a man's world and don't quite know what happened. We've become successful, but it's kind of empty leaving us wondering what went wrong. We've got a great job and everything's working, but somehow there's something missing. The fun has gone because the men are not around. They are not around because we're no longer attractive. They look at women and say, "Wow, she doesn't need me. She's doing everything for herself."

Regardless of how you do what you do, if you're coming from anger it's never going to get you what you want. Men do not improve with abuse. They don't improve with those little hooks and comments that deeply cut and leave scars.

Do not ask what the world needs;
ask what makes you come alive.   Unknown

One of the problems is that women completely underestimate the effect of what comes out of their mouth. They don't know who they're speaking to. They don't realize that who they're really speaking to is a man who is completely willing. He would simply like to know what on God's green earth he can do to make her happy. He's not a mind reader. He can't figure it out by himself. When women get pushy and impatient they drive men further away.

How many times have you noticed that men say, "Well, do it yourself then." They leave and then women get pissed off that they left in the middle of a conversation. She then says, "Well, all I wanted to do was let you know what didn't work for me." This is when the whole breakdown starts.

Women don't realize they could be sitting back and enjoying their life more. They could use more of their feminine energy instead of their masculine energy. I'm talking about her true feminine power; the power she has to attract what she wants in her life by being fully female.

When you are in awe of your own feminine power and have a man who wants to pay attention to you, your relationship can be beautiful and your life a joy. Most women have a man, and what do they do? Club him over the head because he's not doing it right!

When you become a woman again, you no longer need to be in charge of producing everything in your life. You give up the need to do it all yourself, knowing men love to produce and are much better at it. It's in their DNA. Not like women can't do all the things men can do, but men are brilliant at

Today is the tomorrow you were worried about yesterday.
Was it worth it?   Unknown

217

production because they have single-minded purpose. If a woman is committed to doing everything herself, romance will never stand a chance. I met a woman on the airplane who was recently married and told me, "My husband said to me the other day, that sometimes he doesn't know why I married him, because I never need him for anything."

I get so frustrated when I come home and have many things going on in my world that need attention. How do I approach a man for his help?

Simply ask your man to help you with one thing at a time. Men will do many things for you if they experience winning with you. If they're not winning with the one thing you've given them, and you expect them to do more, they just get confused and frustrated. They get frustrated because they're not winning with you. They are thinking, "Nothing I do for you makes any difference, so do it yourself. I'm out of here. I'm going to go watch the Super Bowl. I'm done. This is no fun." How many times have you heard that?

♂♀

There's a way to ask for what you want that works and a way that doesn't. Some things they say can inspire men to brilliant production. You hear "Behind every great man is a great woman". Sometimes it is his wife, but it always is a woman who knows how to operate her man. And you don't operate a man with a crowbar, or inspire him with constant criticism and badgering. That's why I say women underestimate the effect of what comes out of their mouth.

Men are interested in something they can DO and want credit for everything!   John Gray

Women castrate men when they produce everything they want instead of giving a man the opportunity to produce for them. When they allow a man to take care of some of their needs, they not only honor him and his ability to get the job done, but they honor the feminine by receiving his gift.

The world is listening more and more to women every day. It's a very important time. But women have to understand that when they're in charge, they can't say, "Okay, now that we're in charge, we're going to show you guys how wrong you are." This kind of attitude will never bring the world together. Women are the nurturers, the caregivers, the ones who must bring people together. They need to stop making men wrong for the way they've done it in the past.

Men are completely brilliant and capable; the perfect match for women. They are seriously interested in what women want because they know if they aren't happy, nobody is going to win.

Most women think men aren't interested in what they want, because many times men haven't been there for them. It's not that men haven't wanted to give them what they want; it's mostly because women have asked in ways that haven't inspired their production. Their requests in the past have come across like men were wrong and probably wouldn't figure it out. You hear women saying, "If my man really loved me, he would know how to do this." These incredibly insensitive comments make a man feel like he is losing, big time, with his woman. It depresses him and he thinks, "I can't win with her, no matter what I try, so why bother?" Women

Nothing splendid has ever been achieved except by those who dared to believe that something inside them was superior to circumstance.   Bruce Barton

wonder why they leave. When this happens women get to be right about the fact that their man really didn't want to give her what she wanted. Then she leaves in a huff and takes away all the fun. The man then becomes a dullard and looks even more beaten down than he was before she started castrating him. Then a woman becomes even more frustrated that he doesn't want to engage, so she abuses him a little more by continuing to complaining. There's no light at the end of this tunnel.

I'm not saying women are out there with baseball bats, but the bottom line is, women underestimate the terrible effect of what comes out of their mouth. They have no idea of the nature of who men really are. Most men are willing to be total heroes and are ready at a moment's notice to hit the ball out of the park for her. If she would throw him the ball across the plate by telling them exactly what she wants, instead of throwing it into left field, he would hit it out of the park for her and do it every time. If women would give men a chance and not judge how they held the bat, swung the bat or hit the ball, they would be much more empowered to be their hero. This is what a man wants the most. Women judge every tiny detail and men feel it all and say, "Forget it. You hit your own home run. I'm out of here."

Most women don't understand the negative effect they can have on men. I didn't know this either. But as women begin to understand this, they may look at some of their past relationships and realize they have left a lot of devastated men behind. Many of them will look back and think, "Oh my God, what have I done?"

Trust yourself. Create the kind of self that you will be happy to live with all your life.   Foster C. McClellan

When a woman's being an overt playful bitch, she can say much more without having a negative impact on a man because she's being overt about it. She's being responsible for the fact that she's being a bitch. She's fully expressing herself but it doesn't make the guy feel bad, because she's playing with the bitch side of herself, instead of trying to hide it.

Every man knows there's a bitch inside of every woman. Women should give up trying to hide that side of themselves. If women give up the notion that being a bitch is wrong, men won't have a problem with it either. Communications get hurtful and dirty when women don't own who they are; and when they're not responsible for how they're expressing themselves.

A woman can say in a playful and deliberate way, "Hey you, excuse me. Did you see that toilet seat? It's up one more time. Helloooo! Do you know what's going to happen to you? You're going to be cut off. That's right, no sex for a week if you do that one more time." That's bitchy, but it's a playful bitchy. A playful bitch has no intention of doing harm. She just wants to get her point across and be heard.

Remember the movie, *What Women Want* with Mel Gibson and Helen Hunt? He fell into a bathtub and was electrocuted, and for about forty-eight hours could hear women's thoughts. Well, women don't have to dump guys into bathtubs to have them tune into their wavelength. Men don't know what women want, and aren't mind readers. Guess where they look to see how they're doing if women aren't talking? They look at a woman's face. If they're paying

The greatest victory of my generation is that human beings
can alter their lives by altering their attitudes
of mind.   William James

221

attention to her, and she's not talking, all they can do is look at her face to see what's happening. They can walk into a room, and take one quick look at her face, and feel the chilly vibes coming off her. Men are that sensitive. They don't know what on earth to do when she's being chilly. They don't know how to fix it or have it be more fun, but they feel everything.

Men have built-in barometers that tell them if they are winning or losing. They're constantly thinking, "Is this a good thing or a bad thing?" They can see it in a woman's posture. She can devastate a man with a look. And then women wonder why he's not responsive. He's responding, but won't come toward her because she doesn't feel good to him. There's no win here for him.

Unfortunately, for women, everything is written on her face. Her displeasure, disappointment, happiness, joy, ecstasy, boredom and disapproval. It can pretty frightening for men to relate with women. Look around at most women's faces. They're not exactly lit up with joy.

A woman could enjoy driving along with her man on a lovely sunny day, and suddenly think about something horrible and depressing. The vibes in the car will shift immediately. The man will look over at her face and say, "What happened baby? We were having a good time a moment ago and now it looks like some dark cloud just came over you." Men pay attention to a woman's face for most of their clues; they don't know what to do if she's not talking. They say, "What's wrong?" and most women say, "Oh nothing!"

♂♀

A woman provides protection for the most delicate organ in a man, his heart.   Unknown

222

How should a woman tell a man what she wants?

This is a huge piece of the man-woman puzzle. Women are the 'what', men are the 'how'. That's the way man-woman should be played for the most fun. It's the fastest way to fun! But what have women done? They've taken over the man's job and done the 'how'. They tell men what restaurant they want to go to, and then tell them how to drive and where to park, instead of sitting back and enjoying the ride. Let the man do the 'how'. Let him produce. Otherwise there's no victory, there's no hero and there's no game.

Never tell a man what you *don't* want. They are only interested in what you *do* want. Acknowledge what he *is* doing that you like first. Find something right about what he's already doing before you ask him to do something new for you. Otherwise, he'll feel like he's being used. That's what a lot of women do. They tell men what they don't want and leave them with no way to win. Then men just end up feeling bad.

A man once asked me if I had any handouts on how to win with women. You see, isn't that perfect? That's such a guy thing. What does he want? He wants some tools for his tool kit because he just wants to get it right. They want it all spelled out so they can go from A to B to C to D. They know if they simply follow the steps they can win. That's what men want; they want to know *how to* win with you.

What women want will benefit everyone.
Kristina*ism*

It's very evident that women have not been exercising the muscle of asking for what they want. There are a lot of women who are in mystery about their relationships and why there is a shortage of men in their life. They don't quite know what's happened but something is missing. They can't remember what they did in the past to have men be attracted to them. But it's natural and it's who women are. They've just been exercising the muscle of doing it all themselves. They need to start exercising the 'asking' muscle, but in a more playful and fun way.

When I first learned about asking for what I want, our consciousness wasn't as evolved as it is now. We've opened up our hearts a bit more but 20 years ago, I hadn't pursued any real spiritual path, and was operating more out of fear than out of love. I was afraid that I would never really like men. I was a superefficient person who managed many different offices around the US and Canada. I ran around at 90 miles-an-hour not feeling a thing and not needing man. Like many women, I was angry with men. I didn't understand how willing they were or how much they were in the dark about women. As these new understandings unfolded for me, I gained a much greater compassion for men and the spot they are in. Why would women want to hurt men when they just want to be our heroes?

♂♀

It's time to move the energy towards the heart and towards love. Women are in charge because of their huge desire for all the experiences life can offer. Women want a lot, but so much of their wants and desires have been negated. They haven't gotten the attention they want. They're

A woman keeps a man the same way she got him – with approval.   Kristina*ism*

224

not use to letting the world know how much desire they have. They are just beginning to get their 'desire' muscle working. For some, this is the first time in their life that they've given themselves permission to want what they want. Women have felt guilty about what they want, but they need to get over it. Women need to see how vital it is that they speak up, because the things women want are necessary to a more peaceful world. Why? Because the things women want will make them happy.

Can you imagine what this world would look like if all the women in the world were happy? The men would say, "What on earth has happened here? These women are all smiling. My God, they're all happy." Do you know how much peace that would bring to this world? Total peace! Happy women equal happy productive men. With happy men and women, perhaps we could create a new game called "Who wants to be King of Bringing the World Together as One?" That would be a game really worth playing. Women are the ones who will need to inspire men to move in that direction.

The men who are in our lives today are not the men who wrote the rules we all currently live by. Our fathers' forefathers wrote these rules. They didn't take into consideration the feminine feeling, and random nature of a woman. Were they wrong? No. It's simply where the consciousness was at the time. Women have the power to shift the consciousness and have the world be a more joyful and peaceful one by learning to speak up for what they want. Women will be empowered when they learn to trust that the things they want, are only things that will make the world a better place to live.

Come to men with a problem only if you want help solving it. That's what they do. Unknown

Recently, five women and myself were out at a restaurant sitting at a table and this very sweet waiter came over. It was priceless how quickly he became this totally yummy man with the approval of all the women. He would almost run to get what we wanted because we were having so much fun talking with him. We were letting him know what a great job he was doing taking care of us. We were giving him our positive feminine energy and approving of him in a huge way. He couldn't do enough for us. He knew he was making a difference with us and that we genuinely cared about him.

It's so simple to have men become the incredible beings they already are. They are so willing when women are nice to them. When a woman is nice and then wants something from a man on top of being nice, he becomes inspired to be her hero. It doesn't get any better than this for a man. Women have an endless amount of desire. The planet revolves around a woman's desire. Men have desire too, but it's a woman's middle name.

This is a good thing, because one of the most attractive things to a man is a woman who knows what she wants. It gives a man a job to do. They say, "Wow, I could do that for her." They love to do things, especially if they're going to win at the end. ♂♀

When I talk with men who have recently divorced and ask them what happened, they usually say, "I don't know." They don't know what happened because they don't understand women. They just know she's gone. She took her fun away and it all went to hell.

Successful people know fear – but forge ahead anyway.
Holly Stiel

The most powerful way a man can play with a woman is by being OK with the fact that he doesn't understand them. When a man thinks he knows what's going on, he misses the opportunity of being in the moment with her. If a man would show up at her door and see what channel she was on, and paid attention to that, he would win every time. One of my boyfriends use to tell me he always looked forward to climbing the stairs to my place, knocking on the door, and not knowing what channel I was on. He didn't really care, because he knew he would always have fun with whatever channel it was.

With that level of attention, it will always be a fun ride for both of you. Women think attention on them is more fun than anything. When a man's attention is on his woman, she lights up and becomes rather adorable. Both sides always win when women are being adorable.

It's really okay for men to not understand women. When women run into men who think they know women, it's an immediate signal he probably isn't going to be present with her. These kinds of men usually want to control the situation more than relate in the moment. When a man is in judgment of a woman it always suppresses the amount of permission she gives herself to share who she is. The greatest service a man can be for woman is to pay genuine attention to her, be fully in the moment, have no agenda, and be willing to not know what's next.

When a man takes things personally, he becomes work for a woman. Not only does a woman have to deal with her stuff, but now she also has to deal with his fragile ego. This

---

The heart of a woman is what makes the world spin.
Unknown

is exasperating for a woman. And what does she do eventually? It's too much work so she says, "Next!" She checks out. It doesn't work when a man has his ego in the way. It's not a bad thing that every man has an ego, but women really love it when men hear exactly what they have to say and adjust accordingly. Hopefully, they adjust without feeling they are somehow less of a person simply because of her request. If that happens too many times, she will stop talking to him. Instead, she will silently make him wrong. And everyone knows, if a woman's unhappy, there's nothing too silent about it.

♂ ♀

A woman's communication needs to come from her heart if she wants him to truly hear her. It needs to be from a place of love, not from a place of making him wrong or judging him in any way. He knows nothing about what a woman wants unless she informs him.

A male friend of mine was in the dark about why things went awry, and said, "Hey, I have no idea what I did wrong, but obviously I screwed up here. I'm sorry. I'm sure I was a jerk in some way. Would you please tell me what I did, because I have no idea?"

It would be very useful, if men would say something like this because it would give a woman permission to explain what the problem was. She would feel honored and respected because the man trusted she knew where she wanted to go. If he's willing to not know, a woman will usually lead him towards more fun. Women are the ones who are in charge of fun and know where to find it. She needs a man to

You don't get to vote – you already did.
Werner Erhard

get behind who she is and what she wants, in order for the real fun to show up. Women know how the relationship needs to feel to be safe enough to let men in.

♂ ♀

I used to have a lot of male energy. Men used to be scared to death of me. I might have looked like a pretty woman, but I was a ball buster. Victor said he could see it in old pictures of me. I was a center manager with a large seminar company years ago and was a tough cookie. Cute, but tough and hard. I didn't know what there was to know about being a woman. All I knew was that if I wanted to get anything done, I'd have to do it myself. I wouldn't allow a man to do much of anything for me at that point in my life.

Men and women both have male and female sides to them, but women have become much too masculine. The female side of a man is his creative side. Women like it when men show that side of themselves.

Some men would love to have women as friends. It can be refreshing for both sides if they could do the man-woman dance and just be friends. Women would be delighted to have more men friends and men could enjoy having women as friends. No strings, no agendas, no attachments, just being in the moment. Women can have a great connection with a man, even if it's not romantic, if they understand how men operate. Remember, they just want to win and feel like a man. A little acknowledgment and a happy face go along way.

♂ ♀

Creativity springs from the yearning to be
the fullness of who you are.   Ram Dass

If women are living with the background conversation called, 'My life is wonderful', yet their circumstances don't jive with this, then the conversation they're more likely having is, 'There's something wrong'. Men feel this, whether women know it or not.

If a woman believes she's an incredibly juicy, magnificent, powerful woman, she won't care whether she has a man or not. And when she doesn't care and trusts that the perfect things are happening all in the perfect time, a man will have the space to show up. Ever notice how good things happen when you're having a good time simply enjoying your life?

When a woman truly honors the gift of being born a woman, her whole life shifts for the better. It's a big responsibility to be a woman, given that her job is to steer relationships. If they would give themselves permission to be all of who they are, they would have a lot more fun and be much more attractive to everyone, including themselves. When they relate to the circumstances in their lives as if it's who they are, they're not as much fun to relate with.

Women need to learn to relax more, be in the moment, and trust that life is turning out exactly as it should. They simply need to keep their attention on what they want. They will be perfect for the perfect mate. When he comes along, she'll know it. He's only going to come, however, when she gives up worrying about it.

Have fun and love will follow.
Kristina*ism*

The bottom line is, everyone attracts a partner who's vibing at the same rate. Likes attract likes. If you don't like who you're being, then you're vibing at a rate that is attracting someone that probably doesn't like themselves either. When a woman loves who she's being she'll attract a mate of a similar vibration. That will be a fun dance.

People come into our lives for a reason. When a woman meets a man, she doesn't have to immediately surmise that he's not it . No. Ask yourself, what is the lesson here? Why did this person come into your life and how do you want to dance, even if it is only for a day? Every man has a gift as does every woman. Men and women just need to make sure they're not looking for their partner to fulfill them.

Every single man and woman has something extraordinary to offer, even if only for a brief encounter. There's always a lesson. They may be your life partner, or they may be with you a year or two, but there's a lesson every time. If a woman is looking at a man this way, she doesn't have to feel bad about not wanting him for the whole nine yards. Want him for the gift he is in the moment, whatever that is. Then you'll be a woman who can include men in your life for different reasons and different types of relationships. When a woman is being open, kind and considerate, men will be comfortable having her as a friend. And it would be intelligent to have the person who may end up being your life partner, be your friend first. Ultimately, you need to be a friend to yourself first.

Women are best at what – Men are best at how.
Victor Baranco

There are all sorts of amazing men in the world. The men in my life enjoy spending time with me because I'm fun to be with. They don't have to do anything to make me happy because I already am. They can simply be themselves, and they love it.

♂♀

Women must stop making men wrong for the fact that they want to have sex all the time. Most men would like to have it any time that's possible. It would be a good day for them, if between the time the sun rises and sets, he had a sexual encounter with a woman. That would be a really great life for him. Is that wrong? No! Thank God men want it all the time because women don't. Women only want it when they want it. There would not be 6 billion people on this planet if a man's sexual appetite were the same as a woman's.

Men want it all the time, but the smart men know the only sex really worth having is sex a woman wants. The sex a woman doesn't want is never very good. If a man continues to want it when a woman doesn't, he's likely to get it less and less. The best sex happens when women want it because they bring their natural turn on and desire.

Sex that women don't want will many times lead to a physical breakdown in their body. If women don't honor what they want or don't want in the area of sex, they are more prone to get infections. Women get bladder and vaginal problems, because they don't speak up and honor what they want. Too often they allow one more stroke than they really want, because they're afraid of being rejected. They're doing it to be accepted, not because it feels good.

Choose to be awake every moment.
Unknown

232

This conversation is about quality; the quality of relating, the quality of the moment, and the quality that's available everywhere in life. If you want to live a quality life you have to be more present to the moment. Quality relating doesn't happen from a picture of the future that you've created in your mind. It happens when you are fully present and in the moment.

♂♀

Her side of the story, his side of the story.

She says to her girlfriend, "He was in an odd mood Monday night. We planned to meet at a bar for a drink. I spent the afternoon shopping with the girls and I thought his mood might have been my fault because I arrived later than I promised. He didn't say anything about it though. The conversation was very slow, so I told him I thought we should maybe go off somewhere more intimate to talk more privately. We went to our favorite little Italian restaurant where we had our first date. He was still acting a bit funny, so I tried to cheer him up. I kept wondering whether it was me or something else that was bothering him. I finally asked him. He said, "No, nothing is the matter." But I still really wasn't sure.

In the car, on the way home I told him that I loved him deeply and he put his arm around me. I wondered what the hell that meant, because he didn't say it back or anything. We finally got home and I was wondering if he was going to leave me. So I tried to get him to talk but he just switched on the TV. Reluctantly, I said I was going to bed. Then after about ten minutes he joined me and to my surprise we made

The universe is conspiring to make us happy.
Unknown

233

love. He still seemed really distracted. Afterwards I wanted to confront him, but I just cried myself to sleep. I just don't know what to do anymore. I mean, I really think he's seeing someone else."

His side of the story: The Chargers lost. Got laid though.

♂ ♀

Another His and Her Story

Roger is attracted to a woman named Elaine. He asks her to a movie, she accepts, and they have a pretty good time. A few nights later, he asks her out to dinner and again they enjoy themselves. They continue to see each other regularly, and after awhile neither one is seeing anyone else.

Then, one evening when they are driving home, a thought occurs to Elaine and without really thinking, she says out loud, "Do you realize that, as of tonight, we've been seeing each other for exactly six months?" She just thought about it, said it, and then there was silence in the car. To Elaine it seemed like a very loud silence.

Elaine wondered if it bothered him that she said that. She wondered if he was feeling confined by their relationship. She wondered if he thought she was trying to push him into some kind of obligation he didn't want or wasn't sure of.

And Roger was thinking, "Gosh, six months."

And Elaine was thinking, "But hey, I'm not sure I want this kind of relationship either. Sometimes I wish I had a little more space so I'd have time to think about whether I really want to keep going the way we are. I mean where are we going? Are we just going to keep seeing each other at this level of intimacy? Are we heading toward marriage? Towards children? Towards a lifetime together? Am I ready for that level of commitment? Do I really even know this person?"

He's thinking, "So that means it was, let's see, February when we started going out, which was right after I had the car at the dealers, which means, let me check the odometer. Whoa, I'm way overdue for an oil change!"

She's thinking, "He's upset. I can see it on his face. Maybe I'm reading this completely wrong. Maybe he wants more from our relationship; more intimacy, more commitment. Maybe he has sensed even before I have, that I was feeling some reservations. Yes, I bet that's it. That's why he's so reluctant to say anything about his own feelings. He's afraid of being rejected."

Roger's thinking, "I'm going to have them look at that transmission again. I don't care what those morons say, it's still not shifting right. And they better not try to blame it on the cold weather this time. What cold weather? It's 87 degrees out!"

She's thinking, "He's angry. I don't blame him. I'd be angry too. I feel so guilty putting him through this but I can't help the way I feel. I'm just not sure."

Stop thinking about the difficulty, whatever it is,
and think about God instead.   Unknown

He's thinking, "They'll probably say it's only a 90-day warranty, that's exactly what they're going to say, the rats."

She's thinking, "Maybe I'm too idealistic, waiting for a knight to come riding up on his white horse when I'm sitting right next to a perfectly good person. A person I enjoy being with. A person I truly care about. A person who seems to truly care about me. A person who is in pain because of my self-centered, schoolgirl romantic fantasy."

He's thinking, "Warranty! If they want a warranty, I'll give them a warranty. I'll take their warranty and stick it right up their . . ."

"Roger!" Elaine says out loud. "What?" says Roger startled. "Please don't torture yourself like this," she says, her eyes beginning to brim with tears. "Maybe I should have never . . . I feel so . . ." and she breaks down sobbing.

He goes, "What?"

"I'm such a fool!" Elaine sobs. "I mean, I know there's no knight, I really know that, it's silly. There's no knight and there's no horse."

"There's no horse?" says Roger.

"You think I'm a fool, don't you?" Elaine says.

"No," says Roger, glad to finally know the correct answer to something.

Men's testosterone cycles every 20 minutes. If you get into a fight, just wait a few minutes. He will change.   John Gray

"It's just that, it's just that I need some time," Elaine says. Then there's a 15 second pause while Roger is thinking as fast as he can, and tries to come up with a safe response. Finally he comes up with one he thinks might work.

"Yes," he says.

Elaine, deeply moved, touches his hand, "Oh, Roger, do you really feel that way?" she says.

"What way?" says Roger.

"That way, about time," she says.

"Oh, yes." he says.

She turns to face him and gazes deeply into his eyes, causing him to become very nervous about what she might say next, especially if it involves a horse. At last she speaks, "Thank you, Roger," she says.

"Thank you," says Roger.

Then he takes her home. She lies on her bed, a conflicted, tortured soul, and weeps until dawn. Whereas Roger, gets back to his place, opens a bag of Doritos, turns on the TV, and immediately becomes involved with a rerun of a tennis match between two Czechs he's never heard of. A tiny voice in the far recesses of his mind tells him something major was going on back in the car. But he's

---

The immediate now, whatever its nature, is the goal and fulfillment of all living.   Alan Watts

pretty sure there's no way he will ever understand what, so he figures it's better if he doesn't think about it. This is also his policy regarding world hunger.

The next day, Elaine will call her closest friend, or perhaps two of them, and they will talk about this situation for six straight hours. In painstaking detail, they will analyze everything she said and everything he said. They will go over it time and time again, exploring every word, expression and gesture for nuances of meaning, considering every possible ramification. They will continue to discuss this subject on and off for weeks, maybe months, never reaching any definite conclusions, but never getting bored with it either.

Meanwhile, Roger, while playing racquetball one day with a mutual friend of his and Elaine's, will pause just before serving, frown, and say, "Norm, did Elaine ever own a horse?" *

Here's a picture of what we have observed about men:

Men are logical, compared to women.

Men are single-minded, monomaniacal linear thinkers.

Men are success junkies.

Men like to be the cause of things. Have you ever heard a man talk about a date he took a woman on, as opposed to hearing a woman recount it? The man will say things like, 'I took her here and I did this for her and I bought her one of

---

We have a whole culture who is hungry for genuine attention and no one trained to give it.   Unknown

---

* Story By Columnist Dave Barry

these', etc. I did, I did, I did, I did. He's responsible for producing, and he's happy to be the cause. The woman talks about it from being at the effect of his actions. He took me here, he did this to me, then he bought me one of these', etc. I did, I did, I did. He's responsible for producing and happy to be the cause. The woman talks about it from being at the effect of his actions. 'He took me here, he did this to me, then he bought me one of these', etc. He did, he did, he did to me. It's more fun for a woman to be at effect than to be the cause. Women talk about what men did 'to' them; men talk about what they did 'for' women.

Men love cycles: beginnings, middles, and ends. They like a job they can start, work on and complete. A cycle is anything they can start and has an end to it.

Men are relatively slow and dull compared to women.

Men are uninformed about women or where the fun is.

Men gravitate toward fun with no resistance, like a weather vane. Weather vanes don't think about which direction they move, they just move. Men naturally want to move towards fun.

Men speak *man-ese* as opposed to *woman-ese*. When men are talking in a group, each man will take turns talking. Each will add to what the previous man said. When a group of women are talking, they will talk over each other at warp speed, while covering many different things at the

At this time in history, we should take nothing personally. Least of all, ourselves.   Hopi Indian

239

same time. Men discuss one subject and continue on that subject without deviating. They can't understand how women can talk about five or six different things at once.

There could be twelve women sitting around in a circle, talking about everything from new hairdos, to face lifts, to the latest fashions, to their last orgasm. They're tracking each other at the speed of light. They hear each other completely and don't miss a thing that's being said. Their antennas pick up everything. When a man comes into the room, they have to slow the conversation down considerably, because he can't relate to their speed. Most men think it's humorous but don't understand it.

Men are short on approval. They are unacknowledged and unappreciated by most women. You do not hear women ranting and raving about how wonderful men are. You mostly hear them bitching and moaning about everything they're not getting from men. Men are short on all the A words: approval, acknowledgment, appreciation and acceptance. A little bit of approval goes a long, long way. A little bit can turn a frog into a prince instantly.

Men are producers. They want to serve. Their production is insatiable. Society thinks it's the other way around. The myth is that women are the ones who are insatiable. This is not true. Women only want what they want when they want it. They get filled up with life's experiences and are satisfied… for the moment. Men have an insatiable desire to produce and can produce until the cows come home. Notice how many bulls they put in the pasture with all the cows? One bull and twenty, thirty or forty cows. Picture that one. The men

WOMANIUM – Generally soft and round in form.
Boils at nothing and may freeze any time.
Melts when treated properly. Unknown

are the insatiable ones. They can go and go and go. A man's production can provide an awesome life for a woman because they like to have their production used up.

Men set obtainable goals because they want to win at the end. They don't set goals they think are unattainable. Women on the other hand, always say to their man, "Oh, you could do that and then some." Women know that men can produce more than men think they can.

Men are goal oriented. They find many of women's goals to be impractical and frivolous.

Men are in mystery about women.

Men want to make women happy. They come one way - ready and willing.

Men want love and nurturing just like women.

Men are attracted to attractive women. It's all about a woman's attitude. The most important thing is what comes out of her mouth.

Men have a narrow emotional range; from ho to hum. They gravitate toward a steady state. They like it this way. Men don't understand why women like the highs and the lows. Women feel uninspired if it gets too flat. When women are in the car on a trip with a man and gets a little bored, they'll start a fight or an argument to create some kind of motion. Women can feel like they're dying a slow death, if there's nothing going on. Men shouldn't take this personally.

MANIUM – Solid at room temperature, but gets bent out of shape easily. Fairly strong and sometimes heat sensitive.
Unknown

To shift the mood to more fun for his woman he could simply say to her, "Hey, what's the matter, honey? Isn't it exciting enough for you? Do you want to take a break or something? We could pull over to the side of the road and have sex or something, or we could go eat something."

Women like the highs and lows, and men will simply never understand this because they like life to be steady state. Men need to delete "Just calm down, will you?" from their language. Women would calm down if they could but like the excitement of the highs and the lows. Instead of telling them to calm down, look at them and see what's wanted and needed. Women like life to be exciting but sometimes when they're completely out of their bodies, it makes them crazed. When this happens, a big hug will get them back in their body and grounded again.

Men are in mystery why women want so much attention. Women want attention in the worst way. Unfortunately, that's how they get it sometimes, in the worst way. They'd really prefer quality attention to who they are, not just their body. Women are much more than their body and get angry when that's all men pay attention to. They love attention to their body when they know a man appreciates 'who' they are as well.

A man can acknowledge and appreciate a woman, ad nauseam, and then some. Then he can say it all over again. Women love that much attention. A woman's body is equal to a man's car. This is the vehicle they've been given to maneuver through life. It's not the same with men and their bodies. The way a man presents himself is not as important

---

You and I are the force for transformation in the world.
Ram Dass

as it is to a woman. A man can have a flaw in his suit and not know it, or know it and not care. Men do nothing for their appearance compared to women. Look at the trillion-dollar industry women have called 'body beautification'.

Men build muscles to be better equipped to get the job done in life. A woman's body, however, is the main tool she's been given. That's why her appearance is so important to her. Every morning women look in the mirror and notice every new wrinkle or flaw that appears. "Oh my gosh, my car just got a new gray hair, or my car is falling apart." Women were born with the body they have. It's the vehicle they've been given to get them through life. A woman views her vehicle through a lens called, "Am I attractive and compelling enough for a man to want to produce for me for the rest of my life?"

This is really important. A man should never go down the tunnel of making any comment about a woman's 'vehicle', unless it's a positive comment. Even if she says, "Oh honey, how does this dress look on me?" A man would be safe in saying, "Honey, you make that dress look fabulous!" A comment like this or something even more flattering is good. If a man says to a woman, "I don't know about that dress on you, honey," or "do you really like that dress?" he's just blown it. Don't ever go there!

Women must not put the kabosh on a man's production, not on his car, tools, computer, any project he's involved in, or his finances. Whatever men produce is what they want to be known and acknowledged for. Women can acknowledge a man ad nauseam, for what he has produced

---

I am a marvelous housekeeper. Every time I leave a man
I keep his house.   Zsa Zsa Gabor

in the world, but they need to tread lightly on acknowledging his physical body and the way he dresses. If you acknowledge their appearance too much, they will get uncomfortable and a little squirmish. They only took five minutes to get dressed and don't understand what all the fuss is about.

Women love to be acknowledged for anything they wear. Anytime a man does this, he will win with her. Watch a woman light up when a man says, "Oh baby, you look beautiful in that outfit." The acknowledgment has to be genuine and without any hidden agenda to get her into bed. Once she's in bed, you can say, "Honey I love the clothes you had on a few minutes ago, but I like your bare body better."

♂♀

Insights on how to win more with the opposite sex.

We're talking about two things here. We're talking about the dance of man-woman. A way to play, a way to win and a way to have more fun. Men love it when you acknowledge their car or their big truck. Guys are just trucking along. They've got their tool kit in the back and they're on their way to save the day.

Men like to have their production appreciated. Women like to have their appearance appreciated, especially when it's on top of being appreciated for who they are. They want to be appreciated even when they show up on a Saturday morning with a bad hair day, no makeup and warm-ups. Hopefully men know women are still the same person, even

---

The trick in life is to offer what you desperately want to get.
Dalai Lama

when they leave the house without a scrap of makeup on in their sweats. They are still the same valuable human being. It really doesn't matter what women look like. They want to be loved for who they are first and foremost.

If men would take the time to say more about what they see and appreciate about women, they would see how much this makes a woman happy. Men gain big points by giving her quality attention. Simply look at her, notice how she's put herself together and say something complimentary, the more specific the better.

Another way to get points from a woman is to tell her she looks beautiful first thing in the morning. She'll probably never believe you, but this will tell her that you love her au natural. Men don't really care about all the makeup. Men mostly care if she likes herself. If she feels pretty inside because she likes herself, it doesn't matter what she's wearing. If her light's on and she's happy, that's safe and attractive. ♂♀

It's hard for some women to accept compliments. When she doesn't accept a man's acknowledgment, it's because she doesn't think she's okay just the way she is. If a man is going to give her that kind of approval and appreciation, and a woman doesn't already feel this about herself, his words will fall on deaf ears. It's very castrating to a man when this happens. He's trying to tell her how much he likes her 'vehicle' just the way it is and she responds with, "Oh no, oh no."

Men's shoes don't cut, blister, or mangle their feet. Three pairs are more than enough.   Unknown

How many women refuse compliments? Every time they do, they whack a guy. This is mean behavior. It affects the woman much more than the man when she refuses his praise. She's saying no to herself, that she doesn't love herself, so how could a man love her? She's thinking she's not worthy just the way she is. She's also saying God didn't create her as perfect. It's mean and stingy behavior and women do it more than they know. Women have no idea the negative effect this has on men.

A woman rarely works on her 'receiving' muscle. This rips men off from being the hero they so want to be, and from expressing their love in romantic ways. Men are romance waiting to happen. They bring romance to a relationship looking for sex, while women bring sex looking for romance. When men try to be romantic with women by saying how precious they look in the morning, and women don't accept it, they castrate them. When a man can't even tell his woman how beautiful she looks, au natural, or any other way, she's no fun to be with.

Women will respect men more when he doesn't let her lose. However, men should never try to train a woman. All he has to do is get her attention. When a man calls a woman on her negative behavior in a non-judgmental way, women will be able to trust him. It's a woman's goal to be more kind and loving. She appreciates a man who knows and supports her in this way. She appreciates being called on her behavior because she doesn't want to live a life full of ugliness. However, it's easier for her to let go of her stingy ways when a man plays with her instead of making her wrong. This will make her feel like he's not trying to control her.

"Five Minutes" – this is half an hour. It is equivalent to the five minutes that your football game is going to last before you take out the trash.   Unknown

♂♀

One of the ways a man gets in trouble with women is when he has an agenda that disregards what the woman wants. If a man says something nice to a woman and has an agenda attached to it, it won't feel like a genuine compliment. It will always feel like manipulation to a woman. A woman will always feel resentful if she feels like she should reciprocate in some way just because a man has said or done something nice for her. If a man does something nice for a woman, it doesn't mean she should be obligated to dance, to have sex or to do anything. This is very important for men to know and for women to embrace.

♂♀

Men have no idea of the depth of a woman's anger. They don't quite know how it feels for women to have their sisters in other parts of the world forced to wear burkas to cover every inch of their bodies. Men don't realize that women feel a connection with each other. Anytime a man says something that offends the free spirit of a woman she will feel it. Anytime she sees magazines, newspapers, or television that show women being oppressed, she will feel their pain. This is why women love it when men verbalize their genuine concern for women in the world. Women want this kind of acknowledgment and support. They love knowing that men are one hundred percent on their team.

♂♀

You are free in the moment you change your
mind about yourself.   Unknown

Men doubt their ability to produce and women doubt their attractiveness. That's the deal. A woman's world is all about whether she's attractive enough, while a man's is about his ability to have success with his production. That's their hand. Men wake up in the morning wondering if they're going to have a chance to hit a home run, get the job done, and provide for their woman. If a woman is in a relationship with a man, she will wake up wondering if she's going to be attractive enough to have him be interested in her forever.

Men are hungry to fall in love because love inspires their optimum production. When women fall in love they acknowledge, appreciate and approve of everything their man does. They love everything. They love how he kisses, how he's on time, how he takes her to special places, how he calls just to say he loves her, how he sends her flowers when she least expects them, and tells her how beautiful she is. When a woman receives this kind of treatment, she will become inspired to say she loves, appreciates, approves, accepts, and admires everything about him. Most men rarely get this kind of appreciation and acknowledgment from women. But when they do, they feel like king of the world. There's nothing they wouldn't do for a woman including marry her. When he has the appetite and approval of a juicy, happy, gratified and turned-on woman, there's nothing better in the world for him.

Men fall in love and women make deals. Men are just dying to fall in love. For women the deal has to be right. Women are always checking men out. They are testing them

---

Your thoughts, expressions and passions are never a waste –
they are gut-level valuable.   T. Anchorman

248

to see whether they can open them up. Is it going to be safe? Is this man going to honor the things that are important to her?

Men want to adore women, but women have not been very adorable. Men can't adore a woman who runs around acting like a man. They can admire her qualities of maleness, but it's not something they actually want to adore. In reality, women would like to be adored. It's an amazing thing for a woman when he finds her adorable. It makes her feel completely delicious, soft and feminine, inside and out. Women have yet to learn how to be the kind of women that men can adore.

♂♀

Have you heard about the Boy Scout motto versus the Girl Scout motto? The Boy Scout motto is, "I promise to DO my best for God and country"; I promise I'll get the job done. The Girl Scout motto is, "I promise to TRY to do my best." Women will 'try', but men can't count on them, because men wrote the rules and didn't take into consideration the feeling and random nature of women. So women will 'try', but hey, there might be a sale on at Nordstrom's and they're gone! But they will 'try'. That's why men can't count on women to keep their word. If something more fun comes along, or they feel there's another direction they need to go, they will just go that way. And women hate it when men make them wrong for changing their minds. Women can't help it; they just change their mind. It's just plain stupid for a man not to get behind a woman. A man's life would be a lot more interesting if he just said 'yes' to whatever she wants.

Women know the difference between beige, ecru, cream, off-white, and eggshell.   Unknown

Here's how this works. Todd is planning to take Victoria out to her favorite Italian restaurant on Friday night. He's been planning it for weeks. He made the reservations, brought her flowers and shined up his car. He's unaware she's had her eye on the grand opening of a new French restaurant. So they're on their way to the Italian restaurant and he thinks he's about to be her hero. On the way, they drive by some bright lights announcing the opening of the French restaurant. When she see it she says, "Oh my God, the French restaurant is open. Oh, that's so great!" This is a hint. She is saying this because she's hoping he will say, "Honey, do you want to go there instead? We could go there if you'd like, and go to the Italian place another time." What most men do, however, is keep going toward their 'goal' without ever acknowledging her excitement over the new French place. He is hell-bent on going to the restaurant where they made the reservation. Men think they have to complete what they started and miss following a woman's lead to more fun. He'll get to the Italian restaurant and wonder why it's not as fun as he thought it would be.

Men need to learn to follow a woman's lead. If he gives her the opportunity to choose, she will love him for it. No matter where they end up after that it will be a fun experience. She will know he was more interested in her idea of fun than he was in achieving his goal. She will think he's the best and be grateful to have such a flexible man.

When in doubt, buy him a cordless drill. It does not matter if he already has one. They can never have too many.
Unknown

A surefire way to have the best possible evening with a woman is to always find out what she wants to do. It's the most fun way to go because women know where the fun is. She will feel honored by the attention he gives her. The good times will roll.

Men want to be a hero. They can feel when a woman is disappointed.

Men are repelled by a woman's anger. When they see her anger, they know it's only the tip of the iceberg, which frightens the hell out of them.

Men are attracted to women who are winning in life. They're attracted to women who are having a good time. Men will listen to a woman if she's having a good time now. They will follow her anywhere, be happy to open doors for her and do all sorts of gentlemanly things.

A happy, gratified woman is a woman who is getting what she wants. She doesn't sell herself short. She lives from her heart and is 'nice' to herself and others. When a woman's life is good right now, anything a man does for her will be a bonus. An attractive woman is a woman who's happy now. A man looks at her and thinks, "Holy moly, she's already happy. That means anything I do for her is going to be icing on the cake. I can't lose with her." It's safe for men to play with this kind of woman - the happy kind.

Men love to accomplish things. They are brilliant at getting things done. Women can do everything by themselves, but it is way more fun to have men to relate

Men love gifts for their cars. No one knows why.
Unknown

251

with. Simply let men know what you need, give them your energy and approval, and they will become your hero over and over. Men are natural-born heroes waiting to happen.

Men only know what the past women in their lives have taught them. And if women haven't been educating their men about what they want, how would they know? It's sad to say that their main form of education about women has come from the locker room. God bless them for surviving this long in the man-woman game. It's been a tough world for men given all the angry and castrating women there are. Women are not bad and wrong for being this way. It's nobody's fault that relating with the opposite sex has turned out the way it has. But no one has time to sit around feeling bad about what they've done so far. We don't need fixing or any more therapy. There's simply a hand that women have to learn to play. And there's a hand that men have to play, too. When everyone learns how to play their hand more effectively, life will become much easier and a lot more fun.

Remember, men just want to win, so it's really imperative for women to know what they want. This will lead to many opportunities for women to be satisfied and men to be heroes.

♂♀

A fun and revealing exercise for women to do, is to ask several different men for something that they want. All requests must have room for a 'no' otherwise it will feel like a demand. It also works to say 'please' when making the request.

Rope. Men love rope. It takes them back to their cowboy origins, or at least The Boy Scouts. Nothing says love like a hundred feet of 3/8 in. manila rope.   Unknown

Men can ask several different women the following question using these words only: "Is there something I can do for you?" Not, "Can I get you a cup of coffee?" When a man assumes he knows what she wants and he's wrong, then has to refuse his offer. She could be irritated because he forgot she never drinks coffee. This could be another way a man could lose with a woman. Women don't want to have to say 'no' to a man. The most effective way of asking a woman what she wants is, "Is there something I can do for you?" This works well especially if he says her name first.

♂♀

Many times, women don't feel comfortable asking a man for what they want. They feel if they do, they may owe him something in future. This happens a lot to women. They think if a man does something nice for them, they'll need to do something nice in return. In a woman's mind, it seems like the thing men want most is sex. Somehow it will end up going in that direction even when the woman doesn't want it to. Women hate feeling obligated because a man was nice to them. However, they haven't learned to value themselves enough to know they're worthy of his attention and kindness without any obligation. All they need to do is be happy and that's enough for a man to want to give to her.

Women want it all. They have to realize that they can be a huge source of outrageous joy in a man's life because they desire a lot of really fun experiences. They have a difficult time revealing all they want, however, if it doesn't feel safe. If a man is safe, then it's okay to want things. If she feels safe, she can ask for whatever she wants now and more later.

The Three Toughest Questions for Men – What are you thinking? Do you love me? Do I look fat?   Unknown

It's sometimes difficult for men to put attention on women and buy them things for the pleasure of it with no added agenda. Most men have an agenda. They would like to be sexually intimate with women. They are not wrong for this, but where men get in trouble, is when they have an 'attachment' to their agenda. If they don't have an attachment to the outcome, it's no big deal. Women aren't offended as much by this kind of behavior from a man, if there's no attachment. However, when a man has an attachment, women can feel it. It makes her feel uncomfortable to ask him for anything. She ends up not even wanting to ask for a simple, "Would you please open the door for me?" Everybody loses. If women aren't asking for what they want there's no game to play. There's no fun, no joy, and there's definitely no romance.

When men give to a woman because it's the nature of who they are, with no agenda or attachment, they become very attractive to women. When women are compassionate and understanding, they become very attractive to men. A woman can tell a man how she's feels about his agenda without making him wrong. She can say, "You know, I really appreciate your generosity and everything you're doing for me. I want to be your friend and be straight with you. I'm picking up you want more from me sexually than I want to give you at this time. I'm flattered by your attention, but it's just not where I am at the moment."

Women don't need to fix men. They just need to share their feelings in a nice way. A man can't argue with what a woman is feeling. By sharing how she feels, she's not saying he 'did' it to her. She' saying, "I'd like to spend time with you,

Never use "Fine" to describe how a woman looks. This will cause you to have one of 'those' arguments. Unknown

but I keep feeling you want to get me into bed. I need you to know I'm not heading to the bedroom unless it's something I really want. When I genuinely feel you like being with me, it may happen, but not until then." If men will be the honorable guys women know they can be, and put quality attention on women first, they will have much more success at getting their needs met.

Women have been making men wrong for having agendas. This is very ineffective. Most men will tell you, if you give them a chance, that they're always waiting to be made wrong somehow by women. Most men know when they're in a relationship with a woman, it won't be long before she finds something to criticize him about.

In today's world, men are hugely misunderstood. Most women don't have any idea how willing they are. And they don't understand how to play the 'feminine' hand they were dealt with men, either.

Women can always feel when a man has an agenda, just like a man can feel whenever a woman is angry or has something yucky going on. Not every man has an agenda that trumps what the woman wants, but she always feels it when he does.

If you listen to women talking about men, most of them are saying men are wrong because they don't know 'who' women are. Men don't understand women. They've never been able to probably never will.

Realize the shape of your soul is unique - you have
a special destiny here.   Unknown

One of the reasons women are afraid to express what they want, especially around men who they're interested in, is because they think if they say they want something, the man will think he needs to go and get it for her. This makes her feel misunderstood sometimes, because women just love to talk about all the things they love. They don't always have to have them, they just like to consume even if it's conceptually. Women don't want to appear to be gold diggers, so they don't always speak up about what they want around men. ♂ ♀

Sometimes men become offended when women want to hang out 'as friends only'.

The problem usually stems from how she said it, not what she said. She told him what she wanted, which was 'not' him, without first telling him how much she enjoyed having him as a friend. So he immediately feels rejected, and nobody wants to be rejected. Women do this all the time to men because they don't know how to say what they want in a way that he can win too.

Yes, he would love to have sex with you. You're a great woman, why wouldn't he? Maybe he has no agenda. Maybe he'd just like to hang out and get to know you. If you put a man in this box it will usually hurt a him in some way and have him feel very misunderstood. He's with another woman who doesn't understand how willing men are to make women happy.

Behind the façade of your life, there is something beautiful, good and eternal happening.   Unknown

Bless all the men on the planet for being so willing. Women need to realize they are never going to get any smarter, if women are always putting them down for being clueless about the female species. Women need to start communicating from a much more loving place, if they are ever going to educate men about their needs and wants.

It's as simple as saying to a man, "Well, that would be really fun. I'd love to get together with you. I really enjoyed your company the last time we were together. I want to be straight with you though. I'm learning to honor myself and speak up about what I want. I want you to know I would love to go out with you, and right now I'm just looking to have men as friends, and not necessarily have a sexual relationship. I don't want to lead you on. I'm just not sure what you're looking for. If it's a sexual thing, I'm not available. I think you're great, but it's not what I want in my life right now."

That would be a very simple and straightforward way of telling a man what you want. Saying the "friend" word usually clues a man in. Women should practice speaking up and honoring themselves without making anybody wrong. It's simply your truth, right? Right! Another way of saying the same thing would be, "I'm enjoying the fun I'm having meeting great guys like you. I just want you to know though, I'm a woman who goes slow when meeting new men, especially when it comes to romantic relationships." Speak your own truth, without accusing him of anything.

Men don't care if anyone notices their new hair cut. The same hairstyle lasts for years, maybe decades.   Unknown

Women often worry about what a man is thinking. If you're going to worry, worry about yourself. Better still, stop worrying altogether, and say what's on your mind. You are as worthy as the next person. If you're honoring yourself, it can be as simple as saying, "Hey, this is just my truth. It has nothing to do with you. This is just how it is for me. If you still want to go out with me, I'd love to go out with you."

Remember every request needs to include a yes or no for an answer, otherwise, it's not a request it's a demand. When a woman asks a man for something, she needs to give him room to say something like, "No I'm sorry, I won't be able to do that for you, but I'm so glad you asked me."

Women have had a world full of men who haven't had their production utilized, because they've been afraid of them or angry with them. Women have made men wrong forever. With these new insights about the man-woman game, a whole new world can open up. Every single man, whether a woman knows him or not, is an opportunity for more fun. Hopefully women can learn to have more compassion for them, because one thing is for sure, most of men's unsavory behavior comes from being devastated by a woman in his past.

♂♀

One of the things a man really dislikes is having his production wasted. This is the same as a woman getting all dressed up for her man and not being recognized or appreciated for it. The same thing happens every time a woman asks a man to do something for her, and then receives no acknowledgment for it. All men want is a little

---

Slow everything down and assume nothing.
Unknown

'yahoo', 'thank- you', 'you're so good' or, 'I love it.' She can give him a kiss, a wiggle or a squeal. What's even better is to share with her friends what a great guy he is… in front of him. Women need to open up their hearts and mouths and learn to say something nice to men when they do nice things for them. That will make a man excited and eager to do things again.

The same applies to a man. A man's production is as important as how a woman looks when she gets all dressed up. When a woman misses an opportunity to acknowledge a man's production, she misses the opportunity to have him feel more like a man. And if a woman gets all dressed up and a man doesn't notice, it drives a woman crazy. No matter how many times a man sees the woman he's dating or is living with, he would be smart to say something complimentary about how she looks. The same goes for a woman when she is with a man. She should find something about his production, his project or his 'tools' that she can acknowledge. Certainly it can never hurt. It can be disappointing when we go unnoticed.

Women love it when men notice and express what they love about what they see. A lot of guys may notice things, but haven't known how much it means to women for them to verbalize it. Also it hasn't been safe for men to express themselves. Nobody is wrong, men and women simply haven't known what's important to each other.

If you are dependant on one another for worth – you set yourself up for disappointment.   Unknown

Women could learn to receive compliments from men more easily, for the simple reason that they love to be admired and appreciated. Both men and women feel better about themselves when they acknowledge another's kindness. ♂♀

When you understand the man-woman dynamic it can be very exciting. There's so much growth that happens in relating with men and women, especially in the area of self-love.

In order for women to allow themselves to have men do for them, they have to like themselves first. A woman needs to tell a man how much she appreciates it when he gives her quality attention. He needs to know how much of a difference it makes. Men and women can start having a quality of relating that makes it fun to get up in the morning, when they both start giving and receiving more appreciation for one another.

Recently, I was presenting the Man Woman course at a San Francisco hotel. The men at the front desk and bell hops were completely amazed at how much fun my girlfriend and I were having from the moment we walked into the lobby. Everything they did for us we acknowledged with something like, "Oh, you guys are good! We love that! All right!" We were simply happy. Several other happy women friends joined us later. The hotel staff couldn't believe what they were seeing. They didn't know what to think because we were all such happy, appreciative women. The guys were bending over backwards to do whatever they could to make our stay

It is reasonable to want a relationship – it is unreasonable to depend on one to give your life personal satisfaction. Unknown

be the best it could be, because we were so grateful for whatever they did for us. Men everywhere could use more appreciation and approval from women.

When men are cruising through their day and run into a woman who looks like she needs a hand, they can always say, "Is there anything I can do for you?" That's a pretty safe question to ask any woman. She can respond by saying, "Yes, I would love some help with figuring out how this thing works", or, "There's nothing I need at the moment, but I'd love to take a rain check." A woman can say something as simple as that.

The more comfortable a woman is with herself, the more fun she will to be to play with. When people are happy inside, they become people others want to play with.

♂♀

People need to give up making themselves wrong. As soon as they know they've done something that doesn't reflect who they want to be, they can use it as an opportunity to look for what they've learned. Apologize if necessary, and then simply move on. Too many women beat themselves up for weeks on end about something that happened ages ago. How fun is that? Get on with enjoying life now! It could be over before you know it.

We're all doing the best we know how. We're all good people who are simply trying to figure out the best way to have a life. If you want to have more fun, stop judging yourself and lighten up. We have to accept the fact that we are only human. Life is like school. We are here to learn. If we can let

---

Make yourself responsible for every irreplaceable moment.
Unknown

go of the need to have everything mean so much, we can say, "Hey, look what I learned today! Whew, what a day that was! What am I going to learn tomorrow?" Give yourself permission to have more fun with your daily drama; the drama you have chosen. The key word is permission. You are the only one who can give yourself permission to be, do, or have whatever you want.

♂♀

Everyone acts one way around certain people and a different way around others. We think we will be judged. But guess who's judging whom? We are our own biggest judge; positive and negative. Stop judging and decide to fully accept everything about yourself, and you'll find it much easier to be with others. The more real you become with yourself, the more enjoyable your life becomes. Turn up your vibration and bring in more 'joy' to your life. When you are in joy, there's more to enjoy! Just say 'no' to the judge and 'yes' to joy!

♂♀

The priceless gift that all women want is a man's genuine attention. She doesn't need jewels and all kinds of 'stuff'. Baubles are great and they can be fun, but if men think women want what money can buy instead of quality attention, they're totally off track. It's the little things that really mean a lot to women because it demonstrates a man is paying attention. A man's time and attention will always bring more happiness to a woman than anything money can buy.

♂♀

Men are about accomplishment and money. Women are about physical value and connection.   *Unknown*

THREE STEPS TO GETTING WHAT YOU WANT FROM A MAN

There's a way a woman can ask a man for anything. If she asks him in a way that empowers him, he will do anything for her. There are three steps and they are all necessary. *Step One*, the woman needs to find something she loves about him or whatever he's doing. She needs to get his attention in an attractive way. She does this with the tone of her voice and by putting sincere attention on him. When a woman recognizes that a man loves to take care of what she wants, (if they only knew what it was she wanted), relating with them would become a lot more fun. If she has a frown on her face, he doesn't want to talk with her. This could open up something ugly that he would rather not deal with. If a woman wants something from a man, she needs to speak up and say it with a smile and a please. It's sometimes hard for a woman to say please, because it feels like she's beholden to him.

Women can ask a man for anything they want but they have to be having a good time first. A happy woman can easily get a man's attention. Once she has his attention, she continues on to *Step Two* which is to ask for what she wants. *Step Three* is acknowledging the man for whatever steps he takes towards getting her what she wants. *Step Three* is a must or he will feel like his production is being wasted which will leave him feeling very uninspired.

Love is freeware. Be sure to give it and its various modules to everyone you meet.   Unknown

I'm not saying women shouldn't do things for themselves. If she's in the company of a man, however, and wants to have more fun and romance, she will have to express her 'desire' for something. If she's doing it all herself what will she need him for.

Men want to produce. They're born to produce. Women are born with desire. They're very good at desiring. Women are very good at getting the job done too. They're very capable and have proven that. But if women do everything themselves, they lose all chances for romance. There will be no game. There will be no juice. When there's no game, women end up being angry, bitter and resentful. They age prematurely and wonder where all the joy went. If women continue to do it all themselves, they can look forward to being single and right about how wrong men are.

♂♀

Men who point out to a woman that she's doing something wrong, from their ego, instead of their heart, are men who think they can control women. This is a very uninformed man. Men who try to control women never succeed. Women already think they're wrong. They never want to hear from a man that he also thinks she's wrong too. That's why they're stubborn about asking for what they want in a nice way. There's a part of every woman that thinks she's not worthy and that part doesn't want to be nice to men.

A man could say, "Hellooo? Did you like what I just did?" or, "Excuse me, that was mean." or, "That doesn't feel very good." A woman could choose to play with the fact that he

---

Without our tests life would be like
a smoothly paved road to nowhere.   Unknown

264

caught her being mean, and say, "Ooops, caught me. Guess I'll have to say it a little nicer." Then she could say it in a nicer way and he might reply, "Well, that's a little nicer, but I'm not quite inspired to run out and buy you the Hope diamond yet." Then she could say, "Okay, well how about this?" and go for even nicer. If a woman uses her man as her partner and ally in exercising her 'fun' and 'nice' muscles, she will be amazed and at how quickly the relationship will transform.

♂♀

Why did God create us so different? How could men be so uninformed about how life works with women? It's a hard one for women to really comprehend, because men are so brilliant at so many other things. Women think men must understand more than they appear to.

For women to connect with men, it's as simple as exercising the 'nice' muscle. She simply accepts responsibility for the fact that she steers the relationship. Women don't have to change men, they just need to adjust their own attitude and know they are the one in charge of their own happiness.

If people do things because they think they should, instead of because they want to, it'll turn around and bite them. Do whatever you do because it makes you happy. Do it because it brings **you** joy, not only because it makes someone else happy. When people end up being responsible for all their actions, they are freed up to be themselves.

♂♀

If someone loves you, love them back unconditionally. They are teaching you to love and how to open your heart.   Unknown

Women should always try to leave men in better shape than they found them. Many times women want to write men off because of some obnoxious behavior they are usually unaware of. But are men wrong if they are simply one of the millions born in the blue pile who don't understand women? Instead of writing them off women could enlighten them. They could say, "Excuse me, you seem to be a good guy. You probably don't want to repeat what you just did a second ago. It doesn't go over too well with women, and you're too nice of a guy to get on the wrong side of women. You'd win much more if you did something like this instead."

This kind of caring and mentoring that women can do for the men in their lives would do wonders to bridge the gap between men and women. Couples don't need relationship counseling as much as they need to understand their differences. Some people need to work on themselves, but most people are not broken. They just haven't learned to accept that they're only human beings. We are all trying to sort it out. Some are simply more educated about man-woman than others. Singing the song, 'I'm broken and need fixing' is a waste of time. Start putting attention on what works. It's a much faster way to turn things around. When people come from 'everything is good now', more good is just around the corner.

♂ ♀

Men shouldn't do anything for women when it doesn't feel good to them. When a man lets a woman get away with unattractive behavior she'll do it again and won't respect him. She won't respect him because he missed her attack, which tells her she can get away with being mean in the future. She may not consciously know she was being mean,

---

Everything happens for a reason. Nothing happens by chance or by means of good luck.   Unknown

because many women are unaware of how mean their behavior is. It's stingy behavior. She is stingy with her approval and with her acknowledgment and appreciation. Women tend to withhold their gratitude because they are just plain angry. They don't want to have to be nice to get what they want from a man.

When a man lets a woman get away with mean behavior, she doesn't love herself as much. She knows it doesn't feel good to be mean but doesn't know what to say to a man to help her stop this behavior. If a man notices that a woman has done something ugly towards him, it would be smart for him to give her some reality. He can say, "Hey honey, you know I'm here for you and would love to do anything for you. Maybe you could tell me what you want in a nicer way, so I can be inspired to get it for you, instead of being hit over the head with a crowbar." When the woman asks in a nice way he can answer by saying, "Thanks, honey. That's nicer." The man is not making her wrong here. He's just giving her loving reality, understanding that she really wants to be nicer. She'll definitely notice if he says it in a loving way, and this will usually lead to more of what they both want.

If men want to alert women that they're being unattractive, they have to do it from their heart. They can't ever do it from their ego or mind, thinking that they are right, and she's wrong. Women already think they are wrong. If his comment is coming from his ego, it will just make her angry. And men will never win trying to do anger with a

Men are not mind readers and never will be. Their lack of mind-reading ability is not proof of how little they care. Unknown woman. Women have much more to be angry about, especially when you look at what some men are doing to their sisters in the world.

In a recent movie there was a scene in the bedroom where a woman was being mean to a new man in her life. She hadn't decided whether she wanted him or not. He caught her being mean and said, "Why are you not being loving to yourself? Why are you trying to hurt me?" It was a perfect line. He wasn't going to let her fearful, petty and losing ways get in the way of their relating. It was an amazing example of a man who is paying attention to his woman and not letting her lose. She loved it. It instantly shifted her experience of him. In that moment, she knew he genuinely cared about her.

All women have those 'not so pretty' sides to them. This conversation, however, is about accepting each other no matter what. Human beings can't do their lives wrong. The more loving and accepting we are of whatever we've done - the good, the bad and the ugly, the more we become who we are.

Women start, steer, and end relationships

How does a woman start a relationship? She turns on her light. She starts by simply feeling good. Then she may dress up or not whatever makes her feel beautiful inside and out. She chooses to be an invitation for fun. There are many pretty women inside, and they show up when a woman's light is on.

If men ask what is wrong and women say, "Nothing", they will act like nothing's wrong.   Unknown

Women can dress up or put sweats on; it doesn't matter what they wear. Her eyes speak louder than anything. They say to a man, "Yes, if you come over and talk to me, I will not bite your head off. I might be scared, I might be nervous, I might be a little vulnerable, but I am open and I want to play." Men don't come up to women who've got the bitch-from-hell look on their face no matter how pretty they are. If a woman has the 'This is not a good time to approach me' look, a smart man will stay where he is. If a woman is PMSing - Pretty Menacing Stuff, she won't be a magnet for men. If a woman's open for business, she needs to turn her light on by simply smiling. That's all it takes to start.

When a group of women get together all they have to do is say, "Let's go out tonight and meet some men." They'll primp, get all dressed up and turn their engines on. They're hot to trot and have their 'mojos' working. If a group of women turn on and go out to hunt for men they will find men for sure. If men do the same thing and go out thinking, "Let's go meet some girls and see if we can get lucky," they usually strike out and come home drunk. It is not the same thing for men, because they're not in charge of starting relationships. Even a handsome guy who's been around lots of women, and knows how to dance could be unlucky if he's not a woman's want list.

Women start relationships. They don't realize the awesome power they have which is the biggest crime there is in the man-woman game. If women understood they start it all, they would look at men in a whole different way. They'd discover that men are ready, willing and eager to do whatever it takes to make them happy. Men want to play and they're

Ask for what you want. Subtle hints do not work. Strong hints do not work. Obvious hints to do not work. Just say it!
Unknown

269

willing to learn. They'll move a little bit to the left, rub a little lighter, open the door more often; whatever a woman wants. All she has to do is turn her light on, be kind, and let a man know what direction she'd like to go next. Then she simply gives him a smile and a thank you.

She starts and then she steers. How does she steer? By giving him appreciation and approval. A woman steers by knowing what she wants and how she feels. Power steering requires a woman to like herself first. This is a big piece of the puzzle. If she doesn't like herself ,she'll steer the relationship into the ground pretty quick. And no matter what complimentary things a man says to her it won't make any difference to how she really feels about herself. If she wants to be a good driver she must be committed to having a great relationship, which means having it be fun now. She needs to like her man, give him lots of wins, and inspire him to want to produce more for her. If he sees disappointment on her face, the "It's not working", or "You're not good enough", or "You just failed again", look she will be steering the relationship into the ditch.

Sometimes the next thing women do after they've steered it onto the rocks, is get upset about what they did. They don't take any responsibility and then play the 'take away' game. Women get upset and don't realize how willing men are. They think men are not interested in what they want. They take their frustration out on them by saying something mean like, "I'm not going to tell you what you did because I've told you before", or "If you really loved me, you'd know what I want." Women wonder why men leave for another woman. They don't realize they are the one who steered it into the ground.

Women have a very special gift that men don't have. They have this thing called their 'mojo' or 'turn-on'. Women can just look at a man from across a room and turn him on simply by thinking delicious, seductive thoughts. All she has to do is turn up her 'desire' and have the 'I want you look' on her face. When a woman throws this kind of signal in the direction of a man, she will always get his attention. Imagine a man trying to do the same thing. They wish they could. They can try all they want but a woman is just left with, "What is going on with that guy? He's got this really strange look on his face."

If a woman is having a bad day, is in a rotten mood, and doesn't want any attention from her man, no amount of affection from him can change her mind. When women are in a funk they want to stay there until they're done. Even if the guy tries to get her out of it, if she doesn't want to budge, there's nothing they can do to make it better. Men see they can't win and what do they do? They leave, turn on the tube, or go to the fridge and eat. There's little hope for a man to turn a woman around, unless she decides to change her mind and go toward fun.

It's not the same when a guy has a bad day. If his computer just crashed, or his car broke down, or somebody scratched his car, his woman could enter the room with a big smile on her face and everything would instantly change for the better. If she's happy, and says, "Hey honey, I am

The people in your life are not there by accident.
Unknown

271

really happy to see you. I've been waiting for you all day", within a nanosecond his mood will change. He will want to engage with her simply because she's being fun and appreciative. She's happy and that's all that matters to him.

♂♀

Women have this extraordinary power given to them by our Creator called 'turn-on'. It's a surefire way of always being able to get a man's attention. This power is the key to everything. It's the driving force behind a pleasurable, fun life. When women deny they have this turn-on, they miss out on a huge part of what it means to be a woman. Women need to understand the power of this turn-on in order to experience the essence of who they are. When they finally accept they have this power they won't have to be afraid of men anymore.

Back in the caveman days, when men were out hunting the wooly beasts, women had to make them return so they could produce offspring. How many billions of people are there on this planet now? Women had to be able to get their attention somehow. They have the ability to turn-on any time. It's not about using it all the time, but to be in denial that this gift exists is to deny her very essence.

This is the essence of what it means to be a woman. Her turn-on is her desire for pleasurable experience. It's what makes the world go around and produces some of life's sweetest moments. When a woman fully owns this aspect of being a female, she finally comes into her feminine power.

Forgiveness is an act of will – you choose to forgive.
Unknown

This power honors who a woman is and gives her the freedom to be the incredible being all men know they can be. ♂♀

A woman's power also comes from her intuition, her awareness, and her ability to love unconditionally. Her power is best utilized when she communicates from her heart.

The man woman dynamic is perfect because men want to connect too. They want to bond. Being intimate with a woman allows a man to feel more of what a woman feels. Women can connect over anything, but men don't connect as easily. This is one of the unspoken reasons why sex is so important to a man. It allows him to feel the 'oneness' that women can so easily feel with each other.

Women have to be responsible for the fact that they are juicy, turned on, intelligent, spiritual creatures. Women would love men to be happier to relate with them, but men need to learn to love all the wonderful gifts and challenges that come with the 'pink package'.

Women have all the tools and magic of the universe right at their fingertips. They weren't as evolved even seventeen years ago when I first heard these distinctions. It's really an amazing thing to understand how the dynamic of man-woman works. It's a huge gift we've been given. The more we're responsible for it, the more amazing the experiences will be. When women are being responsible for all of what it means to be a woman, men show up a lot more wonderful.

Relationships are about relating in the now, not living in a picture of the future.   Kristinaism

What does it mean to be a responsible woman? A woman is a soft creature, compared to a man. Soft, however, does not mean she has less power. Soft is her power. It's power in a whole new way. Soft and vulnerable, playful and honoring; all acknowledge the essence of a woman.

When women know they have the sex card and understand it's a very special gift, they will learn to use it in much wiser ways. They will use it in a way that's honors and respects the person they're with as well as themselves.

♂♀

A smart way to communicate to someone is to say it from your heart and say, "I feel….", instead of "You make me feel…."

A woman could say, "I notice when I'm dating a man and he shows up late, I feel disappointed and want to shut down to protect myself. I want to give you this feedback because I know it's not your intention to disappointment me." Communicate from your heart in a soft and gentle way, not like anyone is wrong or needs fixing. You're informing him how he could win more with you. Remember that's what men want to do the most. It's hard to argue with how someone feels. If we share from how we feel, it's not usually offensive. A good thing to remember is that your partner is a mirror for you to see where you could be more loving. Be straight, look them in the eye, and speak from a soft and loving heart.

When I meet a new man, I usually tell him, "I'm the kind of woman who will tell you what I need and want. It's always with the intention that you win more with me. It's not about

If love is where you come from, you don't have to look for it.
Kristina*ism*

making you wrong because I'm clear men want to win with women, and they don't necessarily know how to do that. Please don't think I'm the kind of woman who wants to make you wrong somehow. I'm a woman who knows you'd love to make me happy if you only knew how to do that."

A woman sets the tone for her relationships with men. Most men don't know too many women who are willing to be that responsible for being born a woman.

Women end relationships. How do they end it? They take away their approval when he's done something wrong. Women shut the door, and it's over. They say 'no' to their man. This is how simple it is to have a man know she's taken away her approval. When women do this enough men leave. They just respond to the woman. It may look like the man left first, but they only left because she was no longer approving of him. Why should he stick around when he's not wanted? When a woman takes her approval away, he can't win so he will leave.

A woman ends it. It has to be this way because men don't leave relationships that are full of joy, acknowledgment, appreciation and approval. If it's fun why would they leave?

♂♀

Many times women will give a lot of attention towards a man when she isn't acknowledging and approving of herself enough. Approving of yourself makes you attractive. When women appreciate a man too much, he thinks, "This is overkill, it's just too much." It feels weird to the man because

---

he can feel she's not happy about something. She's acknowledging too much instead of letting him know what she wants.

What makes a man happy is when he's with a woman that loves and approves of herself. When a woman loves herself she is happy. This is what makes a man happy; a happy woman. If she is happy he hardly notices that she's not sending approval his way. Her happiness is his acknowledgment. He has somehow produced a happy woman so he's winning. That's all that matters to him.

Most women know they're great in their own minds but don't feel it in their hearts. They don't feel it enough to let it in. When women feel comfortable with themselves from the inside out they can be with men in very intimate ways; ways that don't require words. There is an unspoken knowing of the oneness that exists between the two of you. You feel completely connected to each other with no separation. This is heaven on earth. This is what we're all looking for.

There may be other reasons why men come and go, but there are definitely lessons to learn. It might be interesting to look back and see what you learned from your past relationships. You did not meet by accident. There are no flukes either. Relationships are all about opportunities to learn to become more of who you are.

♂♀

It is a great thing to have someone want to be together and to plunge into pleasures as openly as plunge into the full spectrum of being together.   T. Anchorman

Castration 101

Women may not like what they've heard so far about their responsibility in how their past relationships have turned out. When women begin to discover the kind of effect they've had on men throughout the years, it can be very humbling. Part of the process of learning to own how much power women have, is seeing how they've used it or abused it in the past. This is not always a pretty picture but women need to remember they aren't wrong for whatever they did. If they had known these distinctions way back when, things would have been different. Everything has turned out perfectly so far with the level of knowledge they've had. This is a new opportunity to experience man-woman relationships in a more enlightened way.

All a woman has to do to castrate a man is to simply look at him disapprovingly. What's on her face will affect him that much. If she has a man in her life and is not happy for an extended period of time, she needs to let him know. He will feel responsible for her happiness and wants to fix anything that's broken. If there's nothing he can do to help, she should let him know. She should tell him she'll get back to him when she has sorted it out. This gives him space to do whatever he needs to do, and will also leave him relieved that her situation is not his fault. A woman needs to give him loving reality, because if he's in her life he's affected by everything she feels. He wants his woman to be happy. That's all men want when they have a woman in their life. Of course, if there is something they can do to make her happy, they would love the opportunity.

"Soft Sighs" are one of the things some men actually understand. She is content. Your best bet is to not move or breathe, and she will stay content.   Unknown

There are many ways to castrate a man. "Frontal" castration is the kindest because at least he knows where it's coming from. This is where a woman says something to a man about his car, his business, or anything that reflects his production, which shows she disapproves of it somehow. It could be as simple as saying, "So you like American cars, eh?" or, "Do you really think it's going to work that way?" The purpose is to make him feel bad, and to let him know that she doubts he knows what he's doing. Women don't hear how they sound and are insensitive to the world a man lives in. A man's world is all about production and whether he's succeeding or not.

"Blind spot" castration is when a woman says something nice about what a man has produced for her, and then says something she dislikes about it immediately afterward. She initially fluffs up his ego by saying something nice, making it hard for him to hear the mean thing she adds on. All he knows is that he no longer feels good, and doesn't know what happened.

Women do this all the time, without knowing the negative effect it has on them. He was winning one minute with her approval of how great the evening was, "Gee Honey, I just love eating at this restaurant and I'm so glad you took me here." Then she says, "Too bad the service was so bad." This quickly shifts the mood to one that doesn't feel so good to him. Women can be out with a man and say, "Oh what a gorgeous day. It's so nice that you're taking time off today to be with me", then innocently say, "Too bad it's so hot out." He now feels like he's not winning with her, because she's complaining about the weather. Many women just can't stay

---

*If something men said can be interpreted two ways,
and one of the ways made you sad or angry,
they meant the other one.   Unknown*

278

focused on having a good time. They have to find something to lose about in every situation. Women don't know the effect of what comes out of their mouths.

"Bear trapping", is another form of castration, which happens when a man wants to fix something his woman is complaining about. He wants to produce for her, by fixing it but she continues to give him another obstacle to jump over. She never gives him the opportunity to get it right. He starts in with his solution and she says, "Yeah, but it really wasn't that way". He tries to fix it again with new information from her, and she continues, "No, but it wasn't that way either because..." The guy jumps in again and again trying to make it better for her, and she keeps coming up with yeah-buts. She won't give him any way to win. This is exasperating for a man, making her no fun to relate with. He's thinking, "I'm out of here. Fix it yourself!" He won't want to be around her if he's not given the chance to win.

A better way for a woman to handle a situation like this would be to say, "Okay, honey, I've got some things on my mind and I'd really appreciate you listening. I'll let you know if there's anything I want you to fix. But right now, I just need to get this off my chest. Are you willing to do this for me?" As long as she doesn't intend to attack him, he won't have a problem listening. When she's done she needs to say, "Thank you for listening. I feel much better." He feels like he produced for her by simply listening. It's a win, win. Women don't want to be fixed as much as they want to be heard.

Men see in only 16 colors. Peach is a fruit, not a color. Pumpkin is also a fruit. They have no idea what mauve is. Unknown

An even better alternative is to run any kind of major complaints by your sisters instead of the men in your life. They don't need to hear it and they don't exactly like it, especially if it's about anyone losing.

If a woman is having a problem with something, this is how a man could approach her; first, give her the opportunity to say she wants to work it out. If she doesn't want to, and she's being ugly, and her ugliness is directed toward him, it's a signal to back off. She's not being any fun and it will probably get worse. If it's not the man's fault , she's not going to let him fix it and she's still being mean to him, this is totally castrating and unacceptable.

Women will castrate and sabotage a man until they are heard. She will sabotage his business if she feels he isn't listening. Women can do this in very subtle ways. She can do it through the ethers and through the airwaves. She will do it because she's pissed. She has that much power.

When women are angry about something their man did, even if he was unaware of it, her anger can ruin his day. He can walk out of the house in the morning on the way to a good productive day, and all he has to do is think about the 'hag from hell' he left at home, and his whole day will be clouded by her 'royal ugliness'. Women have that much of an effect on men when they're 'sucking on the gas pipe'. A woman's day will most likely be horrendous as well by this negative behavior. They've been known, however, to cheer up the moment he walks out the door. Their ugly behavior is just to remind him he's failing to make her happy. This is a very lame and painful way to play man-woman.

Slow down. Take nothing personally. Least of all, yourself.
Unknown

Women need to forgive men, for they know not what they do. They need to let a man know what they want, not what they don't want. Never let a man leave your presence with ugly behavior being the last thing he remembers. There's no guarantee he'll return. Really. No one knows what's going to happen from one day to the next. Let's get present and turn up the vibes. Be nice to each other today because you could be history tomorrow. Do you want the last impression you left to be a negative one?

John and I always had a loving good bye when we parted every morning. We lived in England when we were first married. Whenever John left in the morning, I'd go out on the balcony and wave good bye to him as he drove out the driveway. Whenever he left, I truly didn't know if I was ever going to see him again. That was my reality. We always kept total eye contact until he disappeared out of sight. He was left with one happy woman who he was going off to produce for. I knew I was being the best woman I could be. I gave him my love, my appreciation, and my total approval for everything he was doing for me. This always inspired him to have a great productive day. He was going to slay the dragons for his queen. He produced exactly what I wanted. We paid off all our debts and then some. It was an amazing demonstration of how a happy, gratified and appreciative woman can inspire a man to greatness.

John and I rarely had an ugly word between us. Every once in a while I would hang up on him because he was being belligerent. I would call back in a few minutes and say, "Okay, well, you were just being belligerent and I couldn't

What's most attractive to a man is a woman who is happy.
Kristina*ism*

take it any longer." One of us always called back because we never wanted to leave any yucky stuff in the space. We knew life was just too short.

Why Men Grumble

Women castrate men by doubting their ability to produce. When they ask for something from a man, what does he do sometimes? He grumbles. Have you ever heard a guy grumble? They say, "Oh my God, you want what? Oh no, I can't believe it. We can't do that. I can't do that. We don't have that. I don't have the time. I don't have the money." What does a woman do when this happens? She says, "Okay, I'll do it myself, or I'll get someone else to do it. I didn't think you would do it for me anyhow." She'll complain and give up on him and in the process castrate him.

The good news is, the grumbling noise is a man's engine revving up. This is what men do when they look at getting what she's asked for. Yes ladies! This is huge! And this is true! When men grumble, they're looking to see, "Am I going to win here?" It's all about production for them. So what are they looking at? A woman just asked them for something they want and they immediately wonder how can they win? They wonder how am I going to do this? Could I lose here? How am I going to get this done? They're immediately in the mode of trying to figure it out, which they're brilliant at doing. As they do this they start to grumble. This builds their energy to get their engine going. They're planning their strategy. "Oh my God, so she wants this. Hmmmm." They're going through all this noise in their heads.

All men have to do is pay attention – give a woman
that inch, and she will give you a mile.
Kristina*ism*

And what are women doing? They're saying, "I knew I couldn't have it, I'm not worth it, He won't make the time, I knew he wouldn't do this for me." Then she ends up saying, "I'll just do it myself", or she totally gives up on what she wants. By doing this she has cut off any chance for either of them to win. She has choked his engine and castrated him.

Women need to understand the profound impact of this. This is priceless. When a woman asks a man for what she wants, he grumbles. What can she do when he grumbles? She can say, "Oh honey, you're so adorable when you grumble. I just love it. I know you'll figure it out. You're so amazing. You get it done every time. You're the best. You're my hero. You're my man!" This is not manipulation. It's inspiration in the works. A woman can say any combination of the above which will inspire him to do whatever it takes.

When he grumbles after she's asked for something, it means he doubts he can do it. That's what all the noise is about. When a woman doesn't give him any agreement on his doubt, by thinking he won't or can't do it, his doubt disappears. When a woman adds her doubt by saying something like, "Oh yeah, well I guess I really can't have it," you now have two people in agreement about his doubt. With two people agreeing it can't be done, there is now the reality that it can't be done. You both lose. When women sell out on what they want they become miserable and unhappy. He won't get to produce and there will be no chance for him to be a hero. The man-woman game goes out the window. When women become unhappy, dissatisfied, and disappointed with men, they become their worst nightmare. Horrific! And all she did was buy into his grumbling.

The worst judging is judging your Self.
Unknown

God bless men. Let them grumble a little bit. Let them grumble a lot, but play with their grumbling. "Okay honey, well, I know you'll figure it out. I'm going to have lunch with the girls. I'm going to tell them how willing and wonderful you are about getting me what I want. Bye-bye! I'll see you later." When she returns home what is he doing? He was putting his game plan together.

We were living in Seattle. After I did another life-changing seminar in San Diego, I knew I wanted to move there. John and I were married, had a great house, and he had a hobby car; a sexy '67 Cadillac Coupe de Ville. Our seminar business was booming. He thought everything was working just fine, until I brought up the subject of moving to San Diego. His grumbling about the move was really loud. He loved how everything was peaceful and orderly, and now I wanted to uproot everything and move to a new city. I was excited about the move and said in response to his grumbling, "Oh, I know, John, but you'll love San Diego, you really will." I didn't for one minute get hooked by his, "No, oh no," because I knew he would give me what I wanted if I didn't doubt him. He could grumble all he wanted, because I knew deep down that this was going to be the best thing we could do for our lives.

This is not a situation where I am thinking, "To hell with you John. You don't get to have a say in your life." I knew John trusted me enough to know that wherever I wanted to move would be good for both of us. If I didn't know this to be true in my heart, he would end up being unhappy and that wouldn't work for me. I knew myself well enough to trust my intuition. I also knew he would want to share this ride with

Laugh and the world laughs with you.
Cry and you cry with your girlfriends. Laurie Kuslansky

me because I was certain it was going to be fun. Nonetheless, it never would have happened if I had listened to his grumbling.

I came back later that day and what was he doing? He had his note pad out and was downstairs in the basement with his measuring tape. He was measuring all the boxes and everything we had just in case we had to rent a truck to move. He went into high gear before I'd even come home from lunch. Within six weeks, we were living in San Diego. And he loved it. He loved warm weather just like I thought he would.

I want to point out, however, there are a couple of ways men respond. There's the emphatic 'no', and there's grumbling. When it's a complete 'no', you need to listen to that. Why would you want anyone to do something they really didn't want to do? However, if their 'no' doesn't fit with what you know in you heart then you may need to change the form of your relationship. To have anyone do something they don't want to do will not honor who they are.

If a man hasn't had many wins in the past from other women he may tend to be stingy with them. They're leery of putting themselves out there again because they've been hurt too many times before. A woman will have to give a man the experience that she really appreciates all the little things he does. This will allow him to begin to trust that she's not just after his money. Remember it's not your job to fix him. If he's a big 'no' to who you are and what you want, it's probably time to move on.

Some things are good enough on their own not to try to figure them out. If they change, you treat them with the same respect.   T. Anchorman

The top item on a man's want list is for women to be happy. Men don't want the zillion things women want. They simply want women to be happy because they know if they're not, nobody's happy.

Women need to let themselves have material things, because, after all, they are 'material girls'. This doesn't mean men need to go out and buy everything for them. Abundance can manifest in many different ways, but first women need to perceive what they want. Women shouldn't put any attention on what's in a man's bank account before they decide what they want. That's very castrating to him. The things women want can show up in all sorts of ways that don't have anything to do with the amount of money that's available.

I knew a woman who wanted a washer and dryer. She and her husband showed up at a group meeting one night. He announced that they were looking for a set. Her husband said they didn't have the money at the moment to buy them, but his wife wanted them so he was committed to getting them for her. Lo and behold, another man had just received notice from his storage company saying he had to get everything out by Friday. He happened to have a washer and dryer in storage and told the couple they could have them if they could pick them up by Friday. The woman was thrilled. She was happy just wanting it and trusted that her husband would figure out how to get them. He was empowered to produce for her because she didn't doubt him in any way. Just because they didn't have the money didn't mean she wouldn't get what she wanted. He got to be her hero and it didn't cost him a dime.

Wake every morning with the awe of just being alive.
Unknown

Another woman I knew wanted a sapphire ring with diamonds. Her boyfriend knew he was never going to have the kind of money needed to buy such an expensive ring. He put it out there anyhow by thinking to himself, "My baby wants one of these and I'm going to get her what she wants. I'm going to make it happen." A couple of weeks later his friend's mother passed away and in her will left her son a sapphire and diamond ring. This guy new he would never need the ring, but because his friend had told him he was looking for one for his girlfriend the ring showed up.

Everything we want is all around us. It doesn't always have to come from the money we have or don't have. When women doubt they can have what they want because of the current money situation, it's unlikely they will get it. Everyone always ends up with what they truly believe they can or cannot have.

♂ ♀

Women and men can co-produce. Women can buy men lunch, and they can buy them dinner too. Women can buy anything they want for themselves. This particular conversation, however, is about giving men more opportunities to win with women. Some women want to do it all themselves, but this will never give a man the opportunity to be a hero. Women don't want to feel obligated to be nice to men; that's what it really comes down to. They're pissed off at men because in their experience men haven't given them what they want.

Bottom line for women is they've overestimated who they're dealing with. Women think men are a lot smarter about women than they are, and then make them wrong for

To succeed, it is necessary to accept the world as it is – and rise above it.   Michael Korda

not getting it right. Men come one way and that's willing. They just don't know what to do to make a woman happy. Believe me, men get really, really excited when you give them exact instructions as to how they can win with you, especially in the bedroom.

Men are really very simple compared to women. They just want to know exactly how they can win. Women need to tell them the whole scoop about what they want, not just "I would like a new watch for my birthday". You have to tell him 'I want the new gold Movado with the red crystal face and the diamonds around it.' Tell him exactly what you want. That's the only way men get to hit a home run for women.

Women need to ask for what they want, and then savor the waiting by enjoying their life right now. Women need to be having a good time now. If they're not, it won't inspire men to produce anything for them. Some women hold out the fun and sex waiting to see if he will give her what she wants. They've got the club behind their back with an attitude of, "Okay, I told you what I want. Now let's see how fast you can get it done." Men are thinking, "Forget it. I think I'll go to the bar down the street and see if there's anyone there who would be more fun to produce for." Men disappear when women are unappreciative of what they do for them. They will wander off and end up with a woman who appreciates them more. Men don't produce with the crowbar and they don't improve with abuse.

Women need to trust more, and doubt less. When she doubts her man, because it looks unlikely she'll get her goals, and then adds to the doubt by saying, "I bet he's not going

---

Chemistry – two people mindlessly reacting to their hunger simultaneously.   Unknown

to do it", she will lose. He won't do it. It'll be over. He'll feel her doubt. Women can't fool men in this department. He knows when she trusts him and believes he'll get it done. Women should not be impatient. If they're not having a good time now, a man knows they won't be having a good time later. It will be another scenario where nobody wins.

It's all about attitude. What is your attitude about life? A man said to me recently, "It's all about the 'tude'. What's your 'tude'?" A man can say to a woman, "Uh, excuse me. Your 'tude's a little off." If men were playful about it, it wouldn't offend a woman. It would be giving her a little wake up call, a little tap. "Be a little nicer, up the 'tude' and I'll be happy to take you wining and dining."

It's also about a woman trusting and loving herself enough to know she is worthy. If a woman feels she is worthy a man will also think she's worthy. Most of a woman's fear comes from thinking she's not good enough to have what she wants. So instead she projects the blame on the man.

Women have a difficult time receiving, especially when they're not being kind and loving. When they continue to think they're right about how wrong men are, they will end up playing the victim role. This is completely ridiculous because women are the ones in the power position.

♂♀

Personal intimacy requires opening up without defense.
Unknown

Observations About Women

Women self-edit and reduce what they want for two reasons: they doubt their man and they doubt their attractiveness. They self-edit and order short. Women don't need to order short if they trust they'll always get exactly what they want.

Women order by hints and innuendoes. They need to honor themselves enough to ask for what they want, straight out. Women are devious and sometimes covert, because they have low self-esteem.

Women should never get into agreement about a man's doubt. If they deny men reality on the doubt they have about their production, women will get what they want.

Women are trained to settle for less and will always ask for less than what they really want. They think if they ask for too much their man might run. He might think she's being a little greedy and self-centered. However, a woman could stand to be a little more self-indulgent when it comes to pleasure. This is not about being the 'me, me, selfish me'. It's about being someone who takes care of their 'higher self' first.

Women are the random species. They also have the ability to understand the logical, male world. Men are logical, linear creatures and will never understand women. You've probably seen man-woman jokes that tell you 40 different ways to make a woman happy, versus two ways to make a man happy. All it takes to make a man happy is to be a

Shift your attention to what you have.
Ask, what you can offer to the moment?
Unkown

happy woman. Oh, and of course, show up naked and bring beer. Men are easy to understand and they're simple compared to women.

Some women don't know how to let a man know they're happy. Women need to inform their face if they're having a good time. When a man has a woman in his car and she's smiling and happy, he's likely to be moved to say, "You know, you're wonderful to be with because you're always happy. Most women don't smile as much as you do. I'm glad you wanted to go out with me tonight. It feels good just because you're happy."

Women are beings who want what they want, only when they want it. Sorry fellas, but that's the way it is with women. When a woman asks for something, she needs to add her positive energy and enthusiasm to her request. If she doesn't, it won't happen. She needs to inspire her man if he's going to move toward her request.

Place your order attractively to the universe, your man, or whomever. Then go about your life as if everything is on its way. Enjoy the adventure called life and it will be an E-ticket ride.

Men should only produce for a woman if it feels good. Women don't want a man who's pussy whipped, anymore than a man wants to be pussy whipped. What's a turn on to a woman, however, is a man who says 'yes' to her with enthusiasm. When he's a huge 'yes' to what she wants, he will become more attractive to her.

If you want to grow in life and your partner doesn't – it may be a reason to separate. It's not a reason to judge and evaluate.
Unkown

Men are never less manly for giving women what they want. Women love it when men say with enthusiasm and flair, "Honey, whatever you want. I'm your man. I'll not only open that door for you, but I'm going to oil it as well, so you don't have to listen to it squeak anymore." Women love it.

Women worry about being too much work for men. They love it when men enjoy tending to their needs. When men show up this way women become inspired to take better care of men. When they say 'yes' to a woman they are saying yes to a much happier life. It gives them many opportunities to be awesome producers. If they're an enthusiastic 'yes' to women, they'll be juiced in ways that will inspire them to accomplish amazing things. However, when men resist what women want she will take her approval and her juice away.

One of the ways a man can find out what a woman wants is to 'run a menu' for her. He could ask her, "What would you like to do tonight? We could fly to Paris, we can bring in food from your favorite Italian restaurant, I can cook for you, or I can give you a foot rub." Then he should watch her face. When her face lights up simply go in that direction. This is how to win with her. She might change her mind, and if she does, be willing to go in whatever new direction she wants. A man may as well ride the horse in the direction it's going, because women are no fun unless he goes with her flow. If a man is willing to follow her lead, he will be more fun to be with. Doing this for a woman will give him more wins than he ever dreamed. The world has yet to give women all they want.

Respect your own individuality and difference.
Unknown

A woman has to get a man's attention before she asks for what she wants. Then she needs to tell him what she wants and enjoy how he reacts. If he didn't hear her the first time she simply needs to repeat exactly what she said. She must repeat what she said in a friendly manner, being careful not to show any impatience. If she changes how she makes her request, he might get confused about what she wants.

Romance fades when a woman takes on producing what she wants into her own hands. It robs her man of the chance to give to her and compromises the dynamic of man-woman. When a woman simply tells her date what she wants in an attractive way, it will result in a wonderful evening every time. It will be fulfilling because he will be empowered to give her what she wants. In the morning there will be a sweet precious connection that never has to go away.

Men don't always know everything about a woman's happiness, but refusing to accept her suggestions will cost him. It won't be nearly as fun for him as it would be if he were giving her what she wants. When women have what they want they light up. A man who says 'no' to a woman, literally puts her light out. This squashes the essence of who she is which is pure desire. And when a woman's light goes out, it immediately shows on her face and makes her look less attractive. Most men don't understand the effect their 'no' has on a woman.

A man responds to what a woman puts out in every moment. His current state will have a lot to do with whether or not his woman has been approving of him. Men appear much happier when women are saying nice things about

---

Men can quietly enjoy a car ride from the passenger's seat.
Unkown

them and being kind to them. If they look beat up and kind of gray around the gills, most likely they haven't heard anything nice from their woman lately. Women go through their lives and miss so many opportunities to acknowledge and appreciate what their men have done for them. Women's lives are so much better because of men. It can be as simple as finding something she loves about her life and telling him so. She could just say, "Honey, I love our house. I love where we live. It's so beautiful here. Thanks for everything you've done to make this happen." It's the easiest way a woman can let her man know how happy and grateful she is. He'll be in heaven and it won't get any better for him. It's real simple, when men have happy, gratified women at home they will feel like a winner.

♂♀

I told my father, I knew that all he ever wanted was for me to be happy. I told him he succeeded 'big time' with me. I told him life was great and he played a big part in it. I wanted him to know he did a good job raising me. After I told him this it shifted our relationship forever. Anytime we spoke after that day he could hardly keep from tearing up whenever I told him I loved him. He knew I really meant it. He also knew I understood how important it was to him that I was happy. It's real simple to have the men in your life feel like they matter and make a difference in your life.

That's all dad wanted. He wanted to produce for all his girls and make them happy. He had three daughters, a son, and a wife. As each of us married and moved on, he was left with less to do. When all three daughters were married my mother decided to go work, which left him with even less

Men use about 7,000 words per day. Women use about 30,000.
Unknown

to do. The girls stopped needing him to produce for them. Before he passed away I was very grateful I took the opportunity to thank him for getting the job done with me. He knew he had won 'big time' with me. That's all a father wants to do - to see their children happy. That's all any man wants.

If a man dedicates himself to a woman's goals she will support him in every way. As soon as he gets on her side she will be happy. Something magical happens when a man takes on a woman's goals. He will get her endorsement, approval and her energy. There's nothing more powerful than the juice of a happy woman to make the world go around.

Women are called mysterious for many reasons. Men are never going to figure them out, but will keep trying because they want to win. Men shouldn't waste their time and energy on such a hopeless mission. They will never understand women. Much to their disbelief, this is very good news because they don't need to. If he tries to figure her out he'll end up in his head instead of being present with her. If a man would declare, "I don't pretend to know who women are. I don't understand them, I never will, and I'm okay with that", women would love it. They would love a man to show up on a date and say, "Okay honey, what would you like to do tonight? I just want to win with you and I'd like to know what you have on your mind."

A man could start by noticing what's she wearing. That would be clue. Is she wearing any clothes at all? That would be another clue. Is she in the bathtub, cooking dinner, on the phone, reading a book, or meditating? What IS she doing?

Silence, the Final Frontier: Where No Woman Has Gone Before.   Unknown

He could look to see what's she has her attention on and go with that. This would immediately be more fun for her and when it's more fun for her, what does she want to do? Make it more fun for him. When a man is willing to give her this much attention she will always be willing to give back.

Women want to make men happy, too. It's good for women to have men win, because it helps her to feel more loving. Being grateful for all the good in life helps, too. What is life for, other than moment-by-moment nuggets of time to be used positively or negatively? When you're grateful and the love valve opens up, you will be in the flow. Opportunities with higher vibrations will be attracted to you like a magnet. Everything will start to flow when you allow yourself to be in gratitude. If you like something, say it. Otherwise you're missing another opportunity to bring 'feel good' vibes into the moment. ♂♀

What does any man want to do? He wants to hit a home run. He's on a date and wondering whether she's happy and enjoying herself. All he has to do is look at her face to see how he's doing. Is she smiling? Is she having fun? Am I going to get laid tonight? This is what he's thinking.

He's not going to get her into bed if he has an agenda, so he needs to let that one go. He especially needs to drop any attachment to getting laid if he ever wants it to happen. No good and lasting relationship is based on getting laid, it's based on getting connected.

Man Management: Discover How Minor Household Chores Can Wait Until After the Game.   Unknown

Bottom line - men want to know if they are hitting a home run. If a woman likes her date and is having a great time, a man will feel like he's winning and will most likely ask her out again. It's a woman's call. If she's not having fun it will be clear to the man. Men respond to whether a woman was fun by either calling back or not.

Women and Anger

Women are mean and stingy with giving approval. They think if they give too much 'nice' away there won't be enough to go around. This scarcity conversation comes from never feeling completely fulfilled.

Women are mean because they were born second-class citizens. They were born into the men's club. Men wrote the rules. Women feel like they're still treated like a minority.

The worst thing a woman can do is to not give a man reality that she was mean. If she does something mean to him and he says, "Honey, that wasn't very nice," and she denies it. He thinks, "What am I, crazy? That hurt and you're saying you didn't do that?" That's mean behavior when a woman doesn't tell the truth about her intention to hurt him. Sure she was upset about something he did over a week ago, but nothing makes a man crazier than having no reality from a woman on what he's feeling. Giving a man reality is a kind thing to do.

A nicer way a woman can get her communication across would be to say, "I didn't feel heard and that upset me." He then says, "Okay, good. I understand now." And then

Communication Skills: Tears – The Last Resort, Not the First.
Unknown

she says, "Thank you for listening to me". When both of you are heard you can move on. It never works when a woman pretends she wasn't mean. They always feel it when a woman's being yucky. She is more attractive when she owns the fact that she was mean. Men don't have much of a problem with this because they already see it. Her acknowledgment relieves him and he will know he's not crazy.

Women wouldn't be so angry with men if they knew how uninformed they were about women. Just give them your list and they'll get it done. Just don't be mean. It drives men crazy when women are mean. It confuses them and has them not want to do anything. Then it becomes a nightmare. It's a much slower and more painful way to relate when women make guys wrong for being so dumb. They don't know what you want! They are not mind readers! If women believe that men should know, they're in big trouble. A woman's anger around this belief is very counterproductive.

Women get angry when men make them wrong for changing their mind. Women change their minds at least a hundred times a day. Men know women do this but still think women should be different. Because of her rapid changing reality she must never assume a man knows what she wants. She must clearly communicate with him every time. It sounds absurd to a woman that she might have to repeat what she wants three times without changing her words, but this works for men. They are easy to operate if a woman keeps it simple. If she changes the words of what she wants midstream he will think, "Well, that's not quite what she said a moment

Classic Clothing: Wearing Outfits You Already Have.
Unkown

ago." Just say it the same way three times in a row and he will get the picture. This is not rocket science but it is an accurate observation of the way it works.

♂♀

Anger and turn-on have similar physical traits in a woman's body. Both can be very passionate. Turn-on is just a lot more fun. Of the fourteen physically identifiable traits of anger and turn-on, everything's the same except for three additional traits that accompany turn-on. They are 1) pelvic thrusting, 2) lubrication, and 3) engorgement. If you're angry you can quickly shift the anger to turn-on simply by adding a little pelvic thrusting. Soon you will be lubricated and engorged. It's interesting to notice how close they are. This may seem a little unrealistic to shift from one to the other, but you are always choosing, so what are you going to choose? If you're angry you can say, "I think I'll just give this one up and go for some fun. A little bit of pelvic thrusting would be good right about now." Before you know it you will be having a good time.

A woman's anger is exciting and cheap to enter into but very expensive leaving. It's expensive because the residue from a fight can linger for weeks. Sex on the other hand, is only expensive going into it. You may have to deal with the possibility of rejection but there's no exit price tag. It won't cost you anything to have sex and in the end you've both had a good time. You will also got more clear about how to choose fun over a fight.

♂♀

To say that a man loves you is equivalent to saying that they need you. Most men consider that a character fault. It's not easy to admit to one's faults.   Unknown

I live near a Starbucks where five or six firemen would meet regularly for coffee in the afternoon. They always looked very handsome in their uniforms. You know, they're young, they're ready, and they've got their phones close at hand for any emergency calls. One day they were sitting around doing the guy thing. I decided it would be fun to find someway I could let them know that I appreciated who they were and what they did for the community. I was walking by with my coffee in hand, and said jokingly, "Wow, I wish there was a fire at my house." They all thought I very cute to say that. They immediately responded to me with playful conversation and invited me over to their table.

We were talking for about 15 minutes when they discovered I was a relationship coach. They began telling me their fireman stories about women. It was priceless. They were all such good-hearted men; a very special breed indeed. I walked away feeling as though I had made 6 new men friends, and was very happy I chose to initiate a conversation with them.

A few days later I was taking my daily walk and noticed gasoline leaking from one of my neighbor's cars. I knocked on his door and told him to he should check it out. I came back half an hour later and sure enough a fire truck was there. As I was walking around, talking to the owner of the car, I recognized one of the firemen. When he saw me he yelled, "Hey, Kristina!" I laughed and said, "I knew I'd get you guys over here somehow!"

Women come in all sizes, in all colors and shapes.
They are in shape. Round is a shape.   Unknown

Then about two weeks later I was out walking again and a fire truck came screaming up the street with its sirens going full blast. I started jumping up and down, waving away, and giving them the high five sign. They recognized me again and responded with several major blasts on their horn. It was the best! I loved it! They loved it! They were waving and honking their horn. I thought, "Oh my God, that connection with them was so much fun!" I loved that I was willing to be that spontaneous and playful with these amazing and willing heroes. I felt a profound gratitude for being able to understand that at the heart and soul of every man is a hero waiting to happen.   ♂♀

Another example of how women can add fun to a man's life is what I call, "The "Groovy" story. I used to live on a campus of an institute that researched the man-woman dynamic. All the women learned that in order to have a man do anything for them, they simply had to cheer him on and give him lots of wins. This would inspire him to do whatever they wanted or needed.

There was a time when a new gate needed to be installed at the entrance to the property. A large hole about a foot wide and five feet deep had to be dug for the gate post. It had to be dug through hardpan, cement and different layers of blacktop that had been there for years. Whoever was going to dig this hole needed to use one of those big picks, like a pickax, and one of those tools that looks like a huge metal toothpick. This was going to be a helluvah project, and not a lot of fun.

This world is nothing more than a thought you had in heaven one day that was over the minute you had it.   Unknown

John and Dick were asked to tackle the project. Neither of them liked to work this hard, but they went ahead in good humor. My friend Teri and I saw the guys getting ready to dig the hole. We knew this was not going to be any fun for them. Actually it was going to be a total drag because it was 95 degrees out. We watched them as they put the first pick into the ground; it barely broke the surface. We realized it was going to take a long, long time at this rate. We felt for them and knew we could make it more fun, so we started to cheer them on. We yelled, "Yeah! All right! You guys go! Good job! You can do it!"

With the pickax they removed one little piece of dirt at a time. As they made a few more strokes we continued to cheer them on. Within a few minutes of our cheering, a couple of other women came by. Now there were four women cheering them on. It wasn't long before two more guys showed up and said, "Hey, let me do that. Come on, give me a turn." We had four women all doing the cheerleading thing, "Oh, oooh nice muscles!" and then another guy showed up. It was amazing to see the crowd that was forming. We were just having fun acknowledging the testosterone and the men who wanted to win at digging this hole.

John and Dick ended up sitting back under the shade of a tree for the rest of the afternoon, while the other men took turns digging. The women brought music, food and beer. It became a party, it was a 'groovy'. The hole was completely dug four hours later and a good time was had by all. The women turned what could have been a nightmare into a fun project.

I asked God to help me Love others, as much as God loves me. God said....Ahhhh, finally you have the idea.   Unknown

The funniest thing was, it got dug in the wrong spot. They had to dig it all over again the next day because they were eighteen inches off from where it had to be. Even though the whole was dug in the wrong spot, everyone had a good time because of the energy the women brought. They brought the fun. That's what women are good at. Guys will dig any kind of hole, especially when women make it fun.

When I think of men I realize how much I appreciate the physical strength and ability they have to do things like digging holes, paving roads, chopping down trees and fixing broken sewers. They do all the heavy, dirty and smelly work without complaining.

Whenever I see men laboring outdoors, I say, "Yeah! You go guys!" If they're doing landscaping or painting, I say, "Looking good!" This immediately fluffs them up and makes them feel good about what they're doing. They didn't expect to hear this from a woman. When a woman makes these kinds of acknowledgments a man always feels more appreciated. This is fun for a woman to do, especially when she sees their reaction. It makes everyone have a better day and it's so simple to do. Simple, simple, simple!

I never lift my bag into the overhead on airplanes. I wheel my bag on and always know a man will offer to help. I'll just stand there and look as if I need help, and instantly a man will jump up to offer assistance. If not, I'll ask one of the men around if they would please give me a hand. They are always willing. I always genuinely thank them by looking at them in the eye and giving him an appreciative smile. If his wife or girlfriend is sitting next to him, I won't miss the opportunity to tell her, "You have a good one here. He's a keeper."

I want to know what you ache for, and if you dare to dream of meeting your heart's longing. Oriah Mountain Dreamer. Unknown

Think of how much more fun women could be having if they gave men the opportunity to play and win more with them. Most women are angry and upset because they don't think men want to do things for them. That myth goes out the window when the wife sees another woman come by, and without even asking her man, he willingly jumps up to help. His wife is left thinking, "Hmm, maybe I should appreciate him more. He's a really good guy." Hopefully she is left feeling better about her man because he was being a gentleman to another woman who needed some help. When it's time to get off the airplane, it never fails that the same man gets my bag down without me even asking. Let your light shine and appreciate how willing all men are; your brothers, fathers, cousins, friends and acquaintances.

♂ ♀

When you feel good about yourself, it's because you give yourself permission to. Are you somebody who still needs fixing or do you accept yourself the way you are? Some people aren't ready to live that honestly, but it's not your job to fix them. Your job is to love them for who they are. Everyone chooses to live their own truth and all in their own perfect time. When people notice you're being true to yourself, they will enjoy playing with you more. They'll learn to love themselves simply by watching you honoring yourself. This conversation is really all about how much you love yourself.

Ultimately, our life is driven by two emotions, fear or love. When you come from love you attract experiences into your life that resonate with the vibration of love. More people

Everyman needs something where they have complete control, where they are king. Then they are happy to be loyal servants.
John Gray

are waking up and choosing to live with this cleaner conversation. From this place you'll attract a partner who'll match your energy and clarity.

Your level of vibration affects every aspect of your life. It's the underlying conversation you have when you're alone or out in the world. If you're thinking, "What's wrong with me?" you're in the fear mode. There's nothing you have to do or know. You're perfect just the way you are. When you know and fully accept this inside, you will become centered and calm. This is the way to attract good things to your life.

The essence of a woman is desire and attraction. She wants, she attracts, and it happens. It happens when she's at peace inside and trusts the perfection of her life, when she's comfortable with herself. When you can be okay with yourself you won't care what anybody else thinks. You become an example of how much fun a person can be when they love themselves. You're exactly where you should be so give yourself permission to be there one hundred percent.

It's interesting to watch human beings being human. They're all trying to fix themselves to get somewhere other than where they are. This is a problem because it is basically saying, " I am a wrong human being. I'm not quite right. I have to do a little more to fix myself. I've got to lose a little weight or get rid of that, or add on this." Who wants to play with a broken person? How fun is that going to be? If you don't want to be with yourself the way you are, do you think anyone else will?

Men's testosterone cycles every 20 minutes. If you get into a fight, just wait 20 minutes. He will change.
John Gray

When women are completely happy and deliciously delighted with their life, and every moment in it, men will show up everywhere, available and willing. When a woman has her life partner show up, hopefully she will already feel complete and perfect. She must not be coming from lack. When she comes from a place where her life is good now, whatever she wants will show up easily.

Men don't want to be needed by needy women. They want to be wanted by whole and complete women. They want to have their production used in a healthy way. Needy men and needy women are really repulsive and unattractive. Dealing with a person who thinks they are a 'less-than' human being is dealing with a nightmare. It will bring all kinds of manipulation to the relationship which is never any fun. Both parties have to experience themselves as whole and complete first. Then they will have the kind of relationship worth having.

♂♀

Listen-up – I Am Talking To 'You'

The place to come from in life is, 'nothing is missing, it's all perfect'. How could life ever be wrong? Is everyone else's life fine and you are the only one who got a bad deal? People give their power away when they think something's wrong with their life. You're in charge and have been running your life forever. If you want more positive experiences, find what you have now, right. Take a look around and put your attention on what you love about your life, not what you don't like. Be grateful for what you have now. It can be paradise

---

A relationship is something that is given in the realm of commitment and not something exchanged like a bargain.   T. Anchorman

when you need nothing outside of yourself to make yourself happy. Then you'll begin to notice all the wonderful ways to have love in your life.

When you finally know that everything is okay exactly the way it is, it means you also know that everything will come to you in its perfect time. When you accept this as your truth, you will stop the insanity of waiting for life to turn out and become empowered to enjoy the moment.

During one of my workshops a participant thought she wouldn't be complete if she didn't find Mr. Right. I told her, "You need to know in your heart of hearts you'll have the perfect relationship, and then you need to sit back and enjoy the ride right now. Have your light on, share your love and be kind to yourself. You don't ever want to say your life will be incomplete if you don't have a man. That's you not trusting it's going to happen for you. Don't go there. You can say what you want, but if your underlying worry or fear is that it won't happen for you, it won't. Your subconscious mind always ends up being right. You'll end up having what you fear instead of what you want. If you keep putting attention on what you don't want, guess what? You'll end up being incomplete and you won't have a guy."

You will become free when you love and accept yourself. It won't matter whether anyone else loves you because what's important is for you to love yourself. Life will suddenly become much more peaceful. When you love yourself you can see where others don't. You can see a lot more of what's happening around you. If your attention is not on yourself, you will become more useful to others.

There is a discovery of sorts that is worth teaching to others, and there is the peace that comes from being safe and being valued without any effort on your part.   T. Anchorman

What would happen if you gave up the belief that there was something wrong with you? You'd end up knowing you're the one responsible for your life. This would open the door for a new way to relate with people. You could play more with people and the silly ways they judge themselves. In order to do this however, you have to learn play with your own judgments first.

People are so caught up in who they think they are that they miss the opportunity to be themselves. It's fun to go out to a restaurant and just watch people. Many of them are not very present to what's really going on. They appear to have all the right stuff, the cars, the clothes, etc. but their light's not on. They don't appear to be truly happy in the moment. Most people are more committed to looking good than they are to being themselves. It's actually quite funny to watch people doing whatever they're doing as they furiously trying to 'get somewhere'. They are missing one the most important things in life, to be present and enjoy moment.

♂♀

We all have these little 'meat suits' that we run around in. Women have pink meat suits, and men have blue ones. Some have tall ones and some have small ones. But look at how much drama we have over our different meat suits. Start to enjoy and play with how funny human beings are. These meat suits are simply the 'vehicle' you chose to maneuver through life as you learn the lessons you came here to learn. The main lesson being, to love yourself completely so you can love others. That's the game we're here to play. ♂♀

If your needs dominate your mind,
you will have a problem giving.   Unknown

So where are you not loving yourself? Are you giving yourself permission to be the magnificent creature you are? This is it! Your life will only get better to the degree you're willing to have it be good now. I know I've said this a hundred times, but it's imperative to understand this if you want more fun in your life.

When Victor and I got together we knew we it wouldn't be forever because of our 23 year age difference. He wanted kids and I didn't. He asked, "How long will this last?" I said, "As long as it's fun. It could be a week, a month, who knows?" Every time we got together we completely enjoyed each other because we knew it could be our last date. This allowed our relating to be a fresh new adventure every time. Whenever he left he would say, "Bye-bye, that was great fun. You have a wonderful day", and he'd be gone. He'd go out into his world being a whole and complete person doing what he was doing, and I'd be fully into my world. There wouldn't be any drama around needing each other's attention. It didn't exist.

We lived for the moment and always talked about how good everything was. He'd say something nice and I'd say, "Oh, I love it that you said that." Then he'd say, "Well, I love it that you told me that you loved it." And I'd say, "Well, I love it that you told me that you loved it". Then we'd crack up laughing because we were having such fun. We were completely committed to living for the moment. This was one of the greatest gifts I received from this relationship. When you live like there's no tomorrow, extraordinary things will happen to all your relationships.

"Do I look fat?" The correct answer is an emphatic, "Of course not!" An incorrect answer would be, "Compared to what?"   Unknown

♂♀

We've been focusing on the emotional ride women go through. Men have their ride too. They just handle things differently. They keep more to themselves especially if it's not safe. If women choose make it safe for men they will open up and reveal more of their vulnerable side. It's safe for a man when there is no judging or trying to change him.

When women have something really important they need to share with their man they have to get his attention first. She has to be present, real, and vulnerable, so that her man will want to pay attention. Men will be there for a woman when she communicates from her heart. They will feel her because they have feelings too. They're not going to laugh at her if she's being vulnerable. They'll be there without trying to fix her. She can say, "I just want you to hear what's going on with me. There's nothing you need to fix, but if you could just hear me I'd really appreciate it."

In order to have a relationship where each person is acknowledged, fully heard and empowered, each person has to give the other person room to speak. To hear someone completely you need to be present with an open heart. If you're fully present and listening to what they're saying, you won't be waiting for your turn to talk. Each person needs to hear what the other person is saying. This is called 'committed listening'. This makes it safe and will allow each person to learn about each other.

The habits you form while happy are the habits you fall back on when times are tough. Go for the good stuff as often as you can.   T. Anchorman

When a woman's out of her body and talking a mile a minute, it can be frightening to a man. Men don't know what to do when this happens but they know it's not fun. It's actually very abrasive to them. When a woman wants to tell a guy something, he would understand her more easily if she took a deep breath first. This will bring her back into her body and have her feel much calmer. When she's calm and feeling what she's saying, her communication will come across in a totally different way. She will be much more attractive and understandable.

When a woman is crazed it would be good for her to slow down and ask herself what's really going on. What would make her feel better? It might be as simple as, "I think I need a hug. I'm out of my body right now and I feel like crying. Would you please hold me for a minute?" A man wouldn't have a problem with a woman's crying if she was simply being emotional and not attacking him in any way. Crying is like an orgasm. They are both very grounding for a woman. One way or another, a woman will always be happier when she's grounded and present in her body.

Women should save the big emotional outbursts for their girlfriends. Men don't need to experience these. They don't understand half of what's going on in the first place. And if women are not going to let men fix the problem, it's a bad use of their time.

John always knew to put extra attention on me when we were on a road trip. When a woman is in the car with her man she has a captive audience. He can't go anywhere because he's driving. If she's upset with something he did

Respond with joy, and you will have More Joy.
Kristina*ism*

earlier, she thinks this would be a good time to 'work it out'. It might start with, "So, honey?" He'd reply, "Yeeaaah, what?" anticipating the not-so-fun conversation that may be brewing. She might say, "I want to talk about something." Many times instead of honoring herself enough to bring up a subject a nice way, she will say it from the place of being a victim. She will choose to lose and make him the reason why. It's not a fair way to play with a man, especially when he's driving the car without any way to escape.

When I did this with John years ago, he would pull over to the side of the road and call one of my girlfriends (this was before cell phones). He would say to her, "Please just talk to her! She's driving me crazy!" I'd get on the phone and tell my girlfriend how bored I was, how slow it was, and how John was wearing my battery down. We'd talk for a few minutes, and I would get juiced up again. I'd get back in the car and say, "Whew, that was good! Thanks for thinking of that. I feel much better now." I'd be back in the 'nice' mode just like that. That's what women can do for each other. They can connect at any moment and juice each other's batteries. All it takes is two women talking to clear the air.

Guys tend to wear a woman's battery down because they don't have their own juice. They simply respond to a woman's juice. Have you ever been on a vacation with your partner only to find you're in worse shape by the time it's over? If there haven't been any other women around to connect with, it can get pretty dull for her. Women have been known to start fights towards the end of a trip because their batteries are worn down and they need to be recharged.

What you focus on grows – positive or negative.   Unknown

Women have a zillion things going on in their head about everything under the sun, and can't believe that men don't have more on their mind than they do. Women always ask men what they are thinking. This is not to put men down, but men are not usually thinking anything too deep. They're not thinking of much more than what's right in front of them. It's simple for men, it's about pizza, the next football game, a cold beer and how long it may be before they get laid. They are doing the guy thing, being in the zone and praying their woman stays calm and nice.

Women operate with many channels working at the same time. They love to have their women friends to bounce their thoughts off because they know women will always understand. Women can juice other women. They move some of their energy and emotions, which prevents them from torturing men for operating at a slower speed. Sometimes if a woman is bored she'll start a fight just to feel her emotions. Women don't like it when it's too calm. Men wonder why women have so many ups and downs. It's because women like motion and life to be exciting. When it feels too flat they will always find ways to stir things up.

When four guys are driving in a car everyone's happy. There are no problems and they get to where they're going with little or no stress. When there are four women going somewhere in a car, it can be like a three ring circus. They're all happily chatting at 90 mph about everything. There are no rules except that it has to be fun. If they get lost, they are not afraid to ask a man for directions and will then continue on their merry way.

Settle into the world you are in, rather than argue about it.
T. Anchorman

When a woman and a man are alone in a car, a woman can quickly become deeply entrenched in dangerous thoughts, especially if he's not paying attention to her. This will not be a good thing. If they are together for any length of time it would behoove a man to find ways to keep her entertained. Women love it when he does spontaneous and fun things with her along the way. A man who looks for ways to make her happy will always be a winner. Stopping for breaks, sunsets, coffees and shopping will always give a woman the chance to recharge her batteries.

Sometimes men will have an outrageously good time with a woman. They'll have a great dinner, awesome sex, great conversation, lots of laughs and really feel connected. The whole evening could have been special and left on a very high note. Then for no reason, when the man talks to her the next day she's having some sort of nightmare. She's found something to lose about. Women can get outside of their bodies from having a really good experience and if they don't find some way to get grounded again, they will take a downward spiral. They have to get back in their body. Many times they'll create some kind of drama to do this. Balance is what they're after. It's too hard for women to have their life be really good for an extended period of time. They are simply not use to it.

Sometimes women get 'full' from all the pressures in life and just need a break. When they get 'full' they may have what is called 'false appetite'. This is when women pretend to want experiences (like sex) that they really don't want. They think if they stop wanting anything ,a man will wander off. He'll go away and some other woman may get his

---

Connections are great things... real and unforgettable...and they grow on their own, it seems.   T. Anchorman

314

attention. Women rarely let themselves be fully satisfied and gratified. They pretend to want things just to keep a man around and to keep from being alone.

When a woman knows she's full, happy and satisfied and doesn't want anything from her man, she needs to tell him, "I'm very happy and totally satisfied. Everything is really good in my life and you're the reason why. I'm going to take a break for a bit to pamper myself and do some girl things. You've been so good to me you get a hall pass, honey! You can do whatever you want for the rest of the day. I had a wonderful night last night and I just need a break." He now feels completely comfortable about doing his thing. He has reality from her and knows she's in good shape. That's really a great feeling for a man because he no longer wonders whether he got his job done with her or not. He can leave and have a good time knowing he's left a happy camper behind.

John used to love it when I wanted a break. He'd go off and see two or three movies in an afternoon. He'd call me between shows to see if there was anything I needed. I'd say, "No, I'm still happy doing my girl thing." It's always a good thing to give guys reality about how you are doing, especially if it's positive.

One of the mean things women do is when they don't let a man know if he's winning or not. Guys are always wondering what's going on with women and never know what's happening if women aren't talking. A simple, "Yes, I'm good, I'm happy" or "No, this is what I need" relieves a

We do not stop playing because we grow old; we grow old because we stop playing.   Unknown

man from the continual uncertainty he has about his woman. Men like to be in control of their surroundings so it always works for a woman to give him a heads up or a high five.

♂ ♀

What can a man do when a woman is upset? He can start by looking her straight in the eye and say, "Is there anything you need from me? I'm here, and I'm not going anywhere." He can put attention on her by touching or holding her. He can also let her know he loves and adores her. Women want to be acknowledged and appreciated for the difference they make in his life. To verbalize this to his woman acknowledges that he cares about what's important to her. This is a form of intimacy.

That's what women really want the most. The top of their want list is for a man to really listen to her. Women love to be validated by their man. They always love to hear special things that he loves about her. When he let's her know that he appreciates those qualities about her, it tells her that those things are important to him as well. This has a woman feel much more connected to her man and when this happens she feels safe. This kind of appreciation always calms a woman down. It's like giving her a big warm bear hug. It puts her back in her body and all is well.

Women love to know that a man's life is better because she's part of it. Remember the line Jack Nicholson said in the movie As Good As It Gets, "You make me want to be a better man." Well, every woman loved that! They love to see a man's life be more gratified and enriched because of them.

Happiness takes being willing to pay sharp attention.
T. Anchorman

When he acknowledges this he will get big points, more points than he may get by giving her an earth shaking orgasm.

Men sometimes relate to women as if they're messed-up models of men. If a man wants to win with a woman he needs to have fun with where she's at. Men should never try to steer women. It's not a man's job to steer. She's the one who is steering the relationship. The best thing a man can do is get behind her and support wherever she's going. Being with a woman requires paying attention to her. When a man can accept the fact that a woman steers he becomes invaluable to her.

However, a man must not take any 'uglies' from a woman. When there is ugliness being directed toward him, he should address it immediately. He needs to honor himself and not take any yuck from her. A man never wants to reward bad behavior and shouldn't send flowers after a fight that was clearly not his fault. If a man rewards bad behavior she'll know she can get away with it in the future and will respect him less.

Remember, there's always room for an apology. But please never say 'I'm sorry'. Say 'I apologize'. There's a big difference. When you say you're sorry you immediately become a sorry human being. What are you sorry about? Sorry that you did something you intended to do in the moment? No, you meant to do it. It's more powerful to apologize. "Yes, I did mean to attack you, and I apologize. I take full responsibility for what I did. That was mean." It's a much more powerful way of owning what you did. When you

---

Experiences become trivial when you forget to bring the significance to the experience.   Unknown

say 'I'm sorry', you are saying you're a dismal victim of your own actions and you are not responsible. People don't ever have to be victims of their own actions if they know they're in charge of their lives.

♂♀

There is a hierarchy of what women want that comes in three different categories. The most important is called the Sex category, the second is the Food category, and the third is the Baubles category.

The 'Sex' or 'Connection' category is all about attention to her. It's about listening to her, hearing her, feeling her, and then if she wants, it's about having sex. At the bottom of the sex category is intercourse, the least important part of this category. What's more important to a woman is a man's willingness to fully listen to her. She wants to be honored, known, complemented, and loved unconditionally. Then she wants to be romanced, touched, hugged, snuggled, and kissed all the way to delicious orgasms. This is the order of what's wanted and needed in order for her to be truly satisfied. Women want attention to the 'connection' part of this category before a man moves towards sex. The most important thing is for her to feel connected to her partner first.

The next category is called the 'Food' category, which is also known as the 'Survival' category. She wants a roof over her head, good tires on her car, the bills paid, her health insurance handled, and the basic comforts of life taken care of. She wants to feel safe. Handling these things will keep her out of fear.

For attractive lips, speak words of kindness. For loving eyes, seek out the good in people.   Audrey Hepburn

The third category is called the 'Bauble' category. This is the nonessentials category. It includes things like jewelry, flowers, lingerie, shopping trips and fancy dinners. The reason why this is the third category and not the first, as some men think, is because if a woman doesn't feel connected to her man, nothing in the third category will make her happy. If he's not listening to her or paying attention and working late every night, she will never be satisfied. A man will go broke trying to buy a woman's happiness if he doesn't pay attention to her priorities.

It's not that women don't love baubles, but they need to be listened to before baubles will have the kind of effect a man would like to see. After a man has paid attention to the 'Sex' category it's always rewarding to put attention on the other categories. But baubles will only make a woman temporarily happy if she's not getting the quality attention she's looking for.

A man is not responsible for a woman's survival issues unless he's married to her. If he's in a relationship with a woman he can assist her in ways that don't need to be financial. When a woman's planning to get married, it would be smarter for her man to buy her the new mattress she says she needs, before he buys the diamond ring. If she's been complaining about how her body feels from sleeping in a sagging bed, she would love and respect him more if he showed concern for her immediate well being. There's nothing's worse than a woman who doesn't sleep well, and wakes up achy and crabby every morning.

Follow your heart of hearts. Be good to each other.
T. Anchorman

Another example would be a woman's car that needs a tune-up in the worst way. A smart thing for a man to do would be to say, "Hey honey, just because I love you I'm going to get your car tuned up for you." Smarter still, would be, "I'm not only going to get it tuned up, I am going to have it detailed inside and out." This would be much more appreciated than buying her a bauble. If she is worrying about whether her car is going to make it around the next block, a man would be more of a hero if he were to fix this for her. Car issues are not a woman's favorite thing. This will make her feel like he genuinely cares about her and her safety. Women love to feel protected by their man. The 'Food' category is the 'Safe and Secure' category. Emotional safety, physical safety, and then buy her baubles....and lots of them would be just fine and dandy.

♂♀

There are three parts to a simple formula for the 'nice' way to empower anybody to get anything they want from their partner. Men will do almost anything for a woman as long as she asks in a 'nice' way. This is the way where everybody wins.

Step One is to acknowledge something they have done or are currently doing that you genuinely appreciate and love. "You have such wonderful hands. I love how you rub my shoulders." Step Two would be to ask for what you want. "Would you please rub a little harder and keep doing it in the same way?" Step Three would be to acknowledge and appreciate him for any movement he's made towards the request. "Mmm, thank you. That feels just purrfect."

If it had been Three Wise Women, they would have asked directions, helped deliver the baby and brought practical gifts.   Unknown

Think of the three parts to an Oreo cookie. The acknowledgments on both sides of the request have to be made in order to get to the icing in the middle. The first step is finding something about him, or what he's doing, that the woman loves and appreciates. The middle part, the icing, is asking him for what she wants in a 'nice' way. And the third part is acknowledging him for whatever movement he's made toward the woman's goal. Any kind of acknowledgment works with a man. Then she needs to trust it will happen and savor the waiting. She needs to let go and simply enjoy her life. When she's a happy woman, contemplating her wish coming true, he will be inspired to produce for her.

♂ ♀

When a woman wants to bring up a conversation with her man about a serious issue in their relationship there is a powerful and simple way to do it. First take a few deep breaths to calm yourself. A calm woman would get a guy's attention much more easily without him thinking, "Oh my God, here it comes. Fifteen minutes of torture." When a woman is present and in her body a man will automatically be more open to hear what she has to say. She simply looks him in the eye and says, "Have you got a few minutes for me? I have something I'd like to talk with you about that's been on my mind for a while. I want to feel more connected with you, and I think if I can talk with you for a minute it will help."

A woman needs to know any issue she may have will always be her own issue, no matter what she thinks he's done. She simply needs him to listen to her express herself fully. This, in turn, will allow the conversation to open up for

The thing for man to be enthusiastic about is the woman he's with. Victor Baranco, Ph.D.

him to say whatever he needs to say. She can say, "This is how I see it over here. This is what's been going on with me for the past couple of days. I'd like to know how you see it."

The next step is for the woman to be quiet and simply listen to him. She needs to listen fully to make it safe for him. He probably won't tell her the real truth if he knows she's waiting to respond with an attack. After he starts talking, she needs to remember, that what he is saying is his truth. If a woman negates him by not believing what he's saying, it will never work. She can then say, "Well, okay. That's how you see it. Good, thanks for being so honest with me."

If a woman wants to have genuine conversations with her man she needs to be able to accept his truth. Is her goal to be connected or to be right? If she simply wants to be right she'll end up being right… and alone. It's all about listening, enthusiastic listening. It's about allowing his truth to impact her as well, so they both feel heard. A man will talk when he actually feels heard. Women need to be patient. It doesn't mean she has to agree with him or even like what he's saying. Simply allow him to have his truth. Hear his point of view and see if it resonates. Talk like two human beings. Talk and listen and feel each other. If you can do this from your heart there's no reason why you both can't have your needs met. ♂♀

A man is a great barometer for a woman. He can sense the intention behind her words and knows when he's being attacked. Men are brilliant at this. They don't always understand how it became ugly so quickly, but they can feel it in their gut when a woman has an intention to make them

---

The thing for a woman to be enthusiastic about is herself.
Victor Baranco, Ph.D.

wrong. She may not think she's responsible for this but that's because women underestimate the effect of what comes out of their mouth.

It's not just the words a woman says, it's how she says it. She can say cheerfully, "Oh God, what a day!" or she can say sarcastically, "Oh God, what a day!" or dejectedly "Oh God, (sigh) what a day!" They all communicate different things. It's the same words but a different communication. There's a different intention behind them. It's her tone and attitude that makes the difference.

♂♀

If you're coming from your heart, and you know the person you're with is the opportunity to learn more about yourself, you'll realize they're not the problem. You are your only problem. You are the only one who's in the way of what you want. There's no problem outside of you. All the people in our lives are simply there to teach us to be more loving to ourselves.

Do you want to take your life up a notch or down? If you start relating from a loving place you'll have magic happen. It's really easy once you get in the flow of it. It's a much more joyful way to travel in life. It's one of total responsibility. You never have to be a victim. You get to be genuine and real. You can be straight enough to say, "I'm genuinely interested in finding out how we could relate in a more loving way." Know that you're the kind of person who will clean it up if you mess it up. What else can a human being do?

♂♀

Believe in your heart that something wonderful
is about to happen.   Kristiana*ism*

Go toward pleasure each moment and you will be blessed with extraordinary relationships. Choose to have fun with people. They are what make this life worth living. And remember everyone is exactly where they should be, doing the best they know how to do. Every loving thought you have makes life a more loving place to live. It's all your creation. Wake up and smell the roses, or the coffee, or whatever turns you on.

The Beginning!

If you would like to contact Kristina Catalina
or know more about her workshop schedule,
contact her at:

Kristina Catalina
991C Lomas Santa Fe Dr. #422
Solana Beach, CA 92075-2198

or

www.ManWomanMadeEasy.com
Kristina@ManWomanMadeEasy.com

To learn more about Morehouse University, contact:

Lafayette Morehouse
P.O. Box 652
Lafayette, CA 94549
Tel: 925 930 - 6972